SONBLOCK

Sept. 2005

Celia

Continue to live in
the Son's glorious light
Love
Carol

Published by Clear Light Communications Inc.

254 Las Palmas Street

Royal Palm Beach, Florida 33411

SONBLOCK

How Christians Unknowingly Shield Themselves From Grace

Dr. Carol Razza and Denis Eirikis

Cover design by Ana Melissa Cespedes

ISBN: 0-9712299-0-2

Library of Congress Control Number: 2001092848

Your comments on this and all other Clear Light publications are welcome. Please write to address above or email *feedback@clearlightcoms.com*

To order gift copies of this book please call 561/793-5222.

Printed in the United States of America

SONBLOCK

How Christians Unknowingly Shield Themselves From Grace

Dr. Carol Razza
and
Denis Eirikis

communications inc.

www.clearlightcoms.com   (561)793-5222

3

Acknowledgements

Judy Warren deserve thanks and praise for her meticulous proofing and editing of all 743 paragraphs of this book. The authors would like to thank Sister Peggy and all of the Sisters of the Cenacle in Lantana, Florida for providing an oasis of serenity in their retreat house where significant portions of this book were written. Thanks to Linda Lazarus for introducing the coauthors five years ago making this and other collaborations possible. Ana Melissa Cespedes did an exceptional job on front cover design.

Denis Eirikis would like to especially thank my wife Leonor for her patience, love and support. Thanks to my son Mark for his work on the SONBLOCK web site and for making me proud to parent this teen. Thanks Steve for your steady stream of laughs and smiles and for your lighthearted way of reminding me what fun it is to be a dad. Hugs to my daughter Juliet Marie whose kisses and love are all over this book. Thanks Eric Hobbs and Luciana Duce for ministering to me at critical times. But mostly I would like to thank my mom and dad for their encouragement and for the grace they have passed down to me.

Carol Razza. God blessed me over 35 years ago with a safety net that never tears and the wind that has consistently blown beneath my wings always encouraging me to be all I can be, my husband and best friend Paul. I can't go one day without giving thanks to the Lord for our sons Paul and Tim, who have not been, for even a moment, less than blessings in our lives. I love you all.

Contents

This book is the result of four years of prayer and is dedicated to Our Lord Jesus Christ who calls us to trust His love so that we can lower our shields and bask in His grace.

Important Notice:

Throughout this book, in order to better illustrate various points, references are occasionally made to case histories of people that Dr. Razza has encountered during her twenty years of family practice. In order to protect anonymity and privacy, names and details have been changed to such an extent, and composite sketches used, to make it absolutely impossible for the reader to identify any particular person.

Any similarity between the fictionalized names and details of people and incidents mentioned in this book, to any real person, is not representative of reality, but is in the imagination of the reader.

 **Chapter 1**

Let's Take a Walk

"Psychology can take you from misery to unhappiness; God has to take you the rest of the way." Rev. Benedict Rochelle

The deepest part of your insides, the part that cries in the darkness, the part that responds to a child's smile, the part that seeks truth, the part awed by nature, the part that yearns... this is your soul. It's the spiritual being you are, living here on earth in your body, for the time being, as part of God's great and mysterious plan.

Your soul is solar-powered. It runs on only one thing...grace. It always thirsts. You can try feeding that deep yearning inside with sex, alcohol, or material wealth...but these things can be more toxic than nutritious. The soul craves only one thing...God's Light.

If you expose your soul to toxins instead of exposing it to the minimum adult daily requirement of God's healing Vitamin D Sonshine... then it starts hurting, withering, suffering. It aches. In response, you might try to feed it chocolate or maybe buy it a new car or endeavor instead to fix your spouse. You will do whatever it takes to block yourself from the hurt. But in the process, all too many of us block ourselves off from the Light and from each other.

In my twenty years of family practice, day after day good Christians arrive at my door hurting. Most arrive having industriously tried to cover up and protect their hurts, sometimes for decades, in layers of armor. The image that so often comes to my mind is a poor soul trying to hide under an umbrella, even while God's healing grace pours down so freely around them. People inadvertently block themselves from Sonlight. This leaves the soul shaded from grace, malnourished and unhappy.

This book is about identifying the most common types of blocks...and smashing them using God's Word.

The Word offers a very different set of answers and solutions than the world. We all look to the world from time to time, but the problem is that it's so easy to get stuck there without even knowing it. Pretty soon we are busy and fully occupied in the pursuit of money, prestige, fame, sex, and consumer fulfillment. We can no longer see the forest from the trees. We tend to block ourselves off from the Spirit of God. We grow secretly fearful behind our facades and tend to forget that we are His beloved children who need only reach out with our hearts to walk hand-in-hand with the Son.

This book is an exploration of the most common ways we block ourselves off from the SonLight. You are not alone... no one among us is perfect and we all tend to build our little defenses. We co-authors point out our own foibles, our own blocks, and those that we have observed in anonymous patients so that you can better see what might be blocking you. It is only after we take ownership of our walls, blocks, and defense mechanisms that we can ask God's help to smash them down. God wants us to be free and joyful.

Please pay attention to your own issues of trust as you read through this book. I have learned that it is impossible to trust God and to experience fear at the exact same time. More importantly, I have learned that trusting God is a choice. I can choose fear and hiding...or I can choose to trust that God has everything nicely under control.

The idea of *choice* is central to Christianity. God gave us free will. Our fondest hope is that this book will illuminate some of the blocks and obstacles that are stopping you from walking in the fullness of Christ. Once we recognize our blocks, then we have the knowledge and the freedom to make choices about them.

During the final days of writing this book, Den's seven-year-old daughter lovingly brought a strange contraption into his office. She had taped colored construction paper into a kind of crude but beautiful basket, complete with a ramshackle handle. "Here is a God Box for you, Daddy," she said, "Put all your problems down on a slip of paper and put them in here." Even this innocent little child instinctively knew that God is the ultimate healer.

So please keep in mind that this is not a self-help book. It's an asking-God-for-help book. A psychologist cannot nourish your soul. You can't nourish your soul. It's your soul that nourishes you. If you identify and remove whatever is blocking you from the Son, the Light will nourish and heal you on a level that is profoundly deeper than any secular psychologist can imagine.

Chapter 2

Lower Your Shields

Luke 6:41 *"Why do you look at the speck in your brother's eye, but do not **perceive the plank in your own eye?"***

In my nearly 20 years as a family therapist, it never ceases to amaze me how blind we can be to ourselves. As you read stories here about the various blocks your neighbors have built for themselves, instead of marveling at how high their walls nor the nature of their blindness, I invite you to pray for awareness about how your own walk might be less blocked from His grace. *Father God, empower us with Your spirit as we read, become aware of, and take the risk to be all we can be in You.*

I ministered to a family once when I first started my practice. The church had received an emergency call and I had to go to a house where the family had requested help. It was a husband, a wife, and two teenagers - a boy and a girl. Well, they were in terrible shape. The parents and children were yelling and screaming at each other. They were throwing things. I was there for a couple of hours, and finally the situation settled down. As it calmed down, I set an appointment for the next day so that this family could come together and have counseling.

As I was leaving the house, relieved and grateful to the Lord that my first "house call" had gone so well, I decided to inject a little levity and leave them on a lighter note. So I said, "Okay, I'm leaving now. Everything is calm. I'm going to see you tomorrow. We're all going to be at my office and we're going to take care of this. And no one is going to kill anyone, right?"

I was shocked as the wife leered at her husband and said, "The minute you leave, I'm going upstairs and I'm going to get my gun and I'm going to blow his brains out." It was clear that she wasn't joking.

Trying to appear calm, I said, "Oh, do you have a gun?"

She said, "Yes."

So I said, "Get me the gun. I want the gun. I'm not leaving without the gun."

She said, "Well, if I'm giving you my gun, he has to give you his."

I said, "Oh, do you have a gun?"

Then he said, "Yeah, I do."

So I said, "I want your gun too. Get me your gun."

Then he pointed to his beautiful teenaged children and said, "Well, if I give you mine, then they have to give you theirs." Everyone had guns!

Now I am very afraid of guns, but I left the house that day with five rifles, a bayonet, and a handgun. This family was protecting themselves from one another - with guns - with guns! When all they wanted was love. That's all they really wanted. It was a classic example of a defense mechanism…an assumed protection. But it didn't protect them at all. In fact, it kept them away from one another. If I didn't leave with those guns, I don't know what would have happened. She might have blown his brains out. There may have been a little mini-war that would have been good for a minute or two of national news.

> *What we really do is build brick walls around our hearts, which trap us in fear, isolation, and loneliness… we block out the love we so desperately need.*

What is so easy to see in others is often so difficult to see in ourselves. While most of us are much more subtle about it, it's amazing how many of us arm ourselves to the teeth in attempts to achieve protection. In fact, we do this all the time. What we really do is build brick walls around our hearts, which trap us in fear, isolation, and loneliness. When we build walls, we block out the love we so desperately need. As we block ourselves from others, we inadvertently seal ourselves off from the grace and love that God wants us to have.

We are so accustomed to our blocks, we've lived with them for so long, we don't even realize the walls we've built. People will say, "That's just the way I am. That's my nature." Do you ever hear that? "That's just my nature." It eventually becomes our way of life.

When I ask a patient in counseling why they are so fearful or unforgiving or angry, very often I hear, "Oh, that's just my personality." When I hear that I want to scream, "No, it's not!" You were created in the image and likeness of God. This is not your nature. I go wild about

13

this in therapy sessions. People look at me like I'm nuts. They're waiting for me to say, "Oh, yes, that's fine. Does it feel okay? Then keep it that way." Instead I'm saying, "NO! There's something wrong. There's something wrong and it has to be fixed."

When we're fearful or not willing to give up those very things that keep us separated from God, there's something wrong. This book is about looking at what stops each of us - what stops you - from living, breathing, and walking in the fullness of Christ.

I like the imagery of walking in the fullness of Christ because it takes in all the scenery. I imagine walking in God's glorious nature, with the sun shining down, with the birds singing, with fresh air pumping in and out of my lungs and with my legs effortlessly striding along as if by themselves...as if God designed me perfectly to walk in His fullness. We want to walk in His fullness. But what stops us?

I pray that this book will give you a glimpse of the kinds of things that might be blocking you from fullness in Christ and will help you make a decision to let the walls come tumbling down with God's help.

The Facts

First we need to look very briefly at what we need to know about Him, and about ourselves. Do we know, really know, who He is? We can't walk with someone fully if we don't know them. We can only walk superficially. (Can you imagine walking with Christ and limiting discussion to the weather or TV?).

When I take my morning walks, quite often I see other exercise walkers. As I catch up to them, or they to me, we sometimes walk together for a while. We walk together, but we only know each other superficially as fellow walkers. Jesus wants us to know Him intimately. I use this example to contrast the complete intimacy of what it means to walk with Christ.

Jesus doesn't want to have anything come between us. Compare His style of intimacy to the Old Testament temple in Jerusalem. The deepest most intimate place, the Holy of Holies, was sealed off from the common worshippers. They literally built this huge impregnable curtain between God and His children. Now take a close look at the imagery in Luke 23:45, as Jesus died for us, *"The curtain in the sanctuary was torn in two."*

We are now free to enter the Holy of Holies. In fact we are welcomed in with open arms. The Good Shepherd lovingly encourages us to enter that sacred place where, only moments before, only high priests dared tread, and only then on very special occasions. Jesus changed everything.

John 3:16 *"Yes, God so loved the world that He gave his only Son, that whoever believes in Him may not die but may have eternal life."* I have been promised much in my life, but nothing can match God's promise to me of infinite love and eternal life.

Do you know who He is? Do you hear His call? Do you long for the embrace of His arms? Are you drawn to His Light? Do you feel His love?

Having reminded ourselves a little bit about who God is, let us take time to ask, "Who am I?"

The world would probably tell me that I am half way through my life, getting older every day. But God calls me His beloved. In Isaiah, God calls me *"precious and honored."* How about that? The Supreme God of the Universe, more powerful than a locomotive, able to leap tall buildings in a single bound, capable of creating galaxies and solar systems with a flick of His wrist, calls me *"precious."* Who am I to disagree? Imagine the sad folly of trying to build a wall, or arming ourselves to the teeth, against the benevolent and infinite power of God's Love.

We Have to Give Up The Rifles

It's time to give up all the rifles, handguns, bayonets and everything else that you have picked up along the way for protection. Give in to the love in which Your Father wants to immerse you. This will require action on your part... an act of unconditional surrender to the most Holy Spirit.

Surrender is a basic spiritual principal but it goes against our instincts and our egos. Most of us don't like to surrender. Even when self-will has beaten us up and put us in isolation and pain, instead of surrendering unconditionally to God, so many of us instead pretend to sit at a bargaining table with God in an attempt to negotiate the terms of our surrender. "OK, God, I will give up my rifles, BUT You have to do this, BUT my husband has to do that, BUT my kids, BUT, BUT..." When you say "but", it means you are continuing to struggle. Grace, serenity, and joy come as a result of unconditional surrender to The Holy Spirit. Throw in the towel and give up your personal agenda of self will.

We can't know God intimately in the flesh, so He gave us His Spirit. The more we surrender to that Spirit, the more we know Him intimately. We have to surrender to win. This God of creation wants intimacy with His precious ones. It is exactly this intimacy, this incredibly powerful love, that helps us along the journey and that empowers us to overcome the obstacles that arise in our paths.

This book endeavors to describe some of the more common obstacles that block the paths of those souls I encounter daily in my ministry. No one among us walks a saintly path with no briars or potholes along the way. We all have to constantly overcome little blocks created by self. The point is that, no matter the nature of the blocks in our path, we are going to get tired and weary unless we know Him in the depth of intimacy. For me, walking with Him means looking at my choices, my attitude, my behavior, and myself. Can I hold these up to Christ's Light? If not, what stops me?

What stops me? What's my rifle? Usually, we have to notice an obstacle before we are prepared to let go of it. God is going to reveal our particular blocks to us and we are going to put them down. What's still holding us back? What lies are we telling ourselves? How are we protecting ourselves from heartache by discouraging intimacy with family and friends? How are we shielding ourselves from God's grace?

God's Knocking, Open Up!

In order for God to reveal the truth to us, we have to open up that secret box, that dark place within where we hide our pain. I like to call it a "Pandora's Box."

Carl, a friend of mine, is a huge muscular man at around 6'7" and 275 pounds. He looks like a professional football player. One glance at this imposing guy and you would never guess that Carl would have to build walls to protect himself from anyone.

Here's the way he puts it:

"I used to keep my feelings all bottled up deep down inside of me. It was a place that I pretended didn't exist and would never let you near. Because if I put my feelings out on the table where you could see them, I was afraid that you would hurt them."

We need to look inside. We need to look inside and say, "Lord, show me. Show me what I'm blocking." What kinds of things have we bottled up and tried to dispose of by hermetically sealing them inside ourselves?

An image comes to mind that illustrates the point. My kids used to come home from summer camp with these steamer trunks filled with wet, sweat-drenched clothes. God only knows how long the damp clothes were sealed inside those trunks, but the minute I opened the lids, I sure wished they had been left outside in the fresh air and the light of day.

Just like the people who own them, blocks come in all shapes, sizes, and colors. They can affect the body, mind, and soul.

We will see that some of us need healing in our minds. We have been raised to believe things about ourselves that are not true. Some of us need to look at our hearts, to know what is really going on there. Others of us are plagued with soul sickness, are trapped in our family trees, enslaved to our bodies, or are paralyzed in unforgiveness. We will take a close look at all of these things.

With all those secrets and lies bottled within us, we're so afraid to open up. What will I find, Lord? Will I like what I find or will I see that maybe the things that I heard all my life are really true? Maybe I'm not good. Maybe I'm not worthy. Well, in reality, we're not going to find that at all. Because God's saying, "Open it up; have no fear. You're going to find what I created, that precious child that I created. That's what you're going to find."

What's Your Secret Agenda? ... Look for Your "Silent Motivator"

That locked box is a prison. Because anything that is not revealed, anything that is not brought out into the light, is what I like to call a "silent motivator." IT HAS POWER OVER US.

The choices we make, how we view ourselves, and how we interact with other people are all going to be strongly influenced by our silent motivators. Think of it! Our relationship with God, with the people we love, and with our own sense of "self" can all be tainted by the poison of silent motivators, whatever they might be.

We have all heard the expression, "Attitude is everything." It's a critical part of the way I live my life and the way I love my God and allow Him to love me. Silent motivators infect our whole attitude and outlook on life.

That box needs to be pried open. God says over three hundred times in Scripture, "Be not afraid." We don't have to be afraid to find out what's in there. That box that's locked up inside us, even if there are just a couple of things in there, has become a shackle that cripples us on our walk.

I know from my patients that anything left in the box will hamper healthy intimacy. People who carry around invisible but heavy locked boxes don't want to get close to one another or even to God. We say, "Lord, we'll give you so much, but we can't give you everything." So we hold back. We need to know what we're holding back, because most of the time, we don't even know. So that intimacy, that intimate love means, "I must expose my inner self to you, Lord, and in doing that I'm afraid, because what if I find that I really am dirty or stupid?" (or whatever you might say to yourself or believe of yourself.) "Lord, if I find that, then You might not love me."

The truth is that we are all God's beloved. Nowhere in Scripture does God exclude anyone from being called His precious child. So in opening up that box, what we are truly going to find is what God created before the world took us over.

At that moment of conception, God put everything, all of Himself, into us. That's what we're going to find. We're going to find what our gifts are. In Isaiah, it says, *"we were called in the womb to serve."* Well, that means each and every one of us has the gifts, the talents, and all the equipment that we need to do just that. God has a plan for us. So very often we don't live the fullness of that plan. We are all called. We are all gifted.

We need to ask God to search us. We ask Him, "Search me, Lord. Make me acceptable to you." Even though most of us get a little scared about what the answer must be, we must nevertheless ask to grow past the blocks.

The life that God wants us to live is a life that is filled with love. I know sometimes people will say, "That's an idealistic view of life." The world really has distorted us so badly. But Scripture says that we are supposed to live an abundant life.

I remember one man telling me, "You know, you want people then to be perfect." Not me! He does! He does! His word says we should be holy. His word says we should be perfect. Not perfect the way we see perfect, but perfect the way He sees perfect! We need to always be ready to surrender to God, and not to our blocks.

What block stops us from truly embracing these Scriptures and knowing that they're for us? I don't want any of us to try to think about this in the flesh, because God is going to reveal to us exactly what we need to know about ourselves. Some of us, I think, will be pretty surprised. We'll say, "Wow, I didn't know that. I didn't know I was doing that."

God's word is truth and we want to walk in that truth. Whatever it is that is stopping us from walking in that truth, we want to find out. Let's give Him permission to show us.

We're going to look at a number of blocks. I'm just going to touch on them now and then devote a chapter to each.

Trust

Proverbs 3:5-6 *"Trust in the Lord with all your heart. On your own intelligence, rely not. In all your ways, be mindful of Him, and He will make straight your paths."*

Sometimes patients will say to me, "I can't trust. You know, I was raised in an environment where we had to protect ourselves. We couldn't trust one another." or "My first marriage was such a horrible situation that I don't trust anymore. I don't trust men." or "I don't trust women." or "I don't trust anyone." The reality may be that we are not trusting God. We trust our fears, our anxieties. We worry. Our lack of trust in God, manifesting itself as FEAR, is our most common silent motivator and most powerful block.

An Unhealthy Mind is an Obstacle

Romans 12:2 *"Do not conform yourselves to this age, but be transformed by the renewal of your mind, so that you may judge what is God's will, what is good, pleasing, and perfect."*

I ministered once to a beautiful teenager who was afraid to leave her house without wearing a floppy hat and dark sunglasses. Apparently, all her life, the girl's mother had called her "God-awful ugly." After hearing it enough times, the girl believed it and lived her life according to that lie.

This happens to us more often than we might think. If I believe a certain thing about myself, then I'm going to see the world in that way. The mind can be a block. It stops us from receiving that grace upon grace.

How often do our minds dwell on things that aren't good and aren't correct, and in fact, don't build us up, but tear us down?

The Unhealed Heart

I remember speaking at a women's conference and a woman came up to me and said, "I know that the reason why I haven't had any children up to this point is because when I was a teenager I had an abortion. I know that God is punishing me, and He won't give my husband and me children." It was so sad that she believed that this Daddy of hers was punishing her in this way. She couldn't receive His love because her heart was so broken.

Yet, in Psalm 103, God tells us He pardons all our iniquities. He heals all our ills. Sometimes our hearts are so broken from sins that we may have committed or things that may have been done to us. Our hearts are so broken, that we simply cannot believe that we are eligible for God's pardon. We can't hear it. There's a lot to be learned from examining our hearts.

Our Bodies Can Be A Block

Romans 6:16 *"You realize that when you offer yourselves to someone as obedient slaves, you are the slaves of the one you obey."*

Who are we slaves to? Remember the psychology of the sixties? "If it feels good, do it." We believed it, and we continue to do it. Addictions of all kinds run rampant in our society including drugs, sex, alcohol, shopping, cigarettes, food, etc. God is going to reveal to us those obstacles in our bodies that keep us stuck.

23

Our Souls

We don't hear too much about the soul, but an unhealed soul can be an obstacle for living and walking in the fullness of Christ.

I don't know if you've ever questioned, "Where is God? Where is this power that I'm supposed to have in Him?" Have you ever said to yourself, "I'm supposed to be so spiritual, but I don't feel it. Where's the excitement? Where's the abundant life?" When we ask ourselves questions like that, it usually is coming from a soul that needs to be healed, because the soul holds the zeal for God.

Unforgiveness

Colossians 3:13 *"Bear with one another. Forgive each other as soon as a quarrel begins."*

A number of years ago, I was on a prayer team and we were praying for a man who had suffered with pains in his stomach for a long time. He was well into his seventies and said he had the problem for about thirty years. He had been to lots of doctors and they gave him all sorts of medication for it, but the stomach problem persisted. As we were praying, the Lord revealed to us that he needed to forgive someone.

We asked him, "We have a sense that God is asking you to forgive someone. Is there someone in your life that you hold onto?"

He said, "Yeah, I do. But if you knew what she did, you wouldn't forgive her either."

I said, "You know what, I'm sure God is saying you need to give her up."

"Well, it was my sister-in-law -."

"We don't even need to know that. He knows it already. Are you willing to give it up?"

He said, "Yeah."

When he said yes, we began to pray again for his stomach. Then he stood up with a shocked look on his face. The thirty-year-old stomach pain, the unforgiveness of three decades, ceased. He became obedient to the Lord and gave up the unforgiveness, so the pain went away.

In my ministry, I see a lot of physical manifestations that come from holding onto unforgiveness. To blame causes us pain.

Family Tree As A Block

If you take a step back and impartially examine your whole family tree, you will often see conditions passed down from generation to generation. These "conditions" can be positive and manifest themselves as gifts and talents such as creativity or a love of nature. They can also be unhealthy and passed down as negative behaviors and attitudes that block us from walking in the fullness of Christ.

Overcoming Blocks Always Involves Risk

I believe that the Lord is going to speak to us and allow us to zero in on where our blocks are. As we go through this process, we're going to be asked to step out of the boat, to trust Him and to place ourselves in His hands, to leave the baggage behind and walk in His fullness. This book will provide exercises and guides to help you do this. Know as you begin that each Godly risk you take will allow you to know His love more fully.

My prayer for you is from Ephesians 3:14-20 *"That is why I kneel before the Father from whom every family in Heaven and on earth takes its name. And I pray that He will bestow on you gifts in keeping with the riches of His glory. May He strengthen you inwardly through the working of His Spirit. May Christ dwell in your hearts through faith and may charity be the root and foundation of your life. Thus you will be able to grasp fully with all the holy ones the breadth and the length and height and depth of Christ's love and experience this love which surpasses all knowledge, so that you may attain to the fullness of God Himself. To Him whose power, now at work in us, can do immeasurably more than we ask or imagine, to Him be glory in the church and in Christ Jesus through all generations, world without end. Amen."*

 ## Chapter 3

Lonely Distrust

Proverbs 3:5-6 *"Trust in the Lord with all your heart. On your own intelligence, rely not. In all your ways, be mindful of Him, and He will make straight your paths."*

It's hard to believe that the more we give up — the more we gain. To most of us, giving up means loss but the paradox is that the more we give up to God, the more freedom we gain.

You can get a glimpse of this when you imagine giving up worry, giving up booze, giving up smoking, giving up adultery. Imagine, for example, how much we gain when we give up smoking. We gain years to our lives, better health, better breath, and money saved. Yet, we use the language of "giving it up."

When we talk about "giving up" nicotine or alcohol, we are actually talking about "giving up" things like lung cancer and DUI convictions. Of course, most often we are like kids who don't want to give up our 20th candy bar of the day and who don't care to hear a word about tummy aches or cavities. God, our knowing and loving Father, wants us to gain freedom.

I work with so many who struggle each and every day with worry. Will I have enough money to support my family? Will I ever retire and enjoy my life? Will my husband be faithful? Will my children be safe? Even though worry is bad for our health and no amount of worry can improve the chances of favorable results, so many of us worry. God wants us to give it up.

A healthy faith journey allows us to grow in trust and gives us the freedom to live and enjoy today knowing that whatever happens in life... God will turn it around for good.

Rom 8:28 *"We know that God makes all things work together for the good of those who have been called according to his decree."*

Let's do a thought experiment. Imagine that Bill Gates, President Bush, and the Pope have known you since birth. They all love you very much and they have promised to help you however they can. Think of it! No more money worries. The next time you have a money crunch and need an extra million, your buddy Bill Gates has agreed to help out. The President of the most powerful nation that the earth has ever seen wants to be your pal and has placed the entire military at your disposal. Meanwhile, the Pope has agreed to be your spiritual advisor.

With friends like these, would you still worry so much?

Now imagine something infinitely better. Your Father is the Supreme Creator of the Universe who has enough power in His little finger to create billions of galaxies, each with millions of stars. Imagine the power. Feel the power! Now imagine that your Father loves you more than any parent has ever loved any child. Feel the love. I can just imagine Christ asking us why we worry so much.

I have the wonderful opportunity everyday to journey with people in spiritual direction and counseling. I have learned so much from these wonderful brothers and sisters that have shared their pain, as well as their joy, with me.

I remember one broken man who was referred to me by his pastor. His wife was having an affair and it was unclear whether she would remain with him or leave. He couldn't live with the uncertainty. He asked her to leave, after a friend confided to him that he saw her out to dinner with another man.

When confronted, his wife finally admitted to the affair and she left the marriage shortly thereafter. Then she did even more hurtful things. She tried to convince their grown children that she had never loved their father. She instructed her divorce attorney to try to get custody of the kids, the house, and even the business that her husband worked in alone.

As time went on, she became more and more aggressive. His overwhelming hurt turned into anger and quickly moved toward hate. He became locked in the prison where so many people who seek therapy find themselves. He wanted to find a way to get even with her and started exploring ways to destroy the house and the business before they became hers.

He was angry with God. "God, how could you let this happen, I trusted you." What he didn't understand was that God is not a puppeteer. In fact, his wife's free will choice was not God's doing, but her own. The trust that he thought he had in

God was based on trying to control God rather than experiencing His Grace through all of life's situations.

Only when he was able to really digest the Scriptures and let their truth nurture him, could he rise above the anger and hate he was feeling towards his wife. He would sit, sometimes for hours, in the church to soak up all he could from the spirit of God who loved him so much. He read the truth and surrounded himself with a community of believers that would love and support him. He learned that to trust really means knowing that, whatever happens, Jesus will give you the strength to carry on.

On a side note, his fear of losing everything, including the love of his children, never came to pass. His trial brought him further along the journey and allowed him to know, without a shadow of a doubt, that God's will for his life was not destruction....but life to the fullest. I don't want this to sound like an easy road, it's not, but this route allowed him to mature in his faith. He learned to do exactly what Christ calls us to do, to die of self, so that we can be reborn of the Spirit.

Death of Self Will

Father Benedict Rochelle, in his book <u>Spiritual Passages</u>, says: "Only an adult commitment to faith, which implies the death of self, can deliver the thinker so that he or she can become a lover of truth."

That phrase, "death of self," sometimes frightens us. It has a connotation of loss, because death normally is loss. In the Word, God tells us differently. He told us we needed to die of self. Since He said it, it has to be something worthwhile. The way the world labels or defines "death of self" is going to be a whole lot different than the way Jesus defines "death of self."

Self will and ego will not help us make spiritual progress. Are we going to listen to the world...or to Jesus?

Rochelle goes on to say, "The childish impulse to control God by prayer and works and the attempt of the adolescent mind to control Him by speculation and understanding must come to an end."

We spend a lot of energy trying to control God in our prayers. Don't we? "Oh, Lord do this, please do that, heal this one this way, let this one live, let this one die in peace, let this one win, let this one lose." In other words, we are trying to talk God into bending His will to ours, rather than the other way around.

We try to control Him. When we don't get the answer that is obedient to our will, we think God didn't answer us. How many of us say, "God hasn't answered my prayers. I just pray all the time and He never answers my prayers." We never really look at what He is teaching us in the process. Because if God loves us all of the time, then He is involved with everything that happens to us. We have to have faith that no matter what happens to us, God will use it for good, if we allow the good to happen.

Pain is the Touchstone of Progress

He is always teaching us. If you are like me, you'd like to have a day off every once in a while to just vegetate, but He is always beckoning us towards fullness. Sometimes the only way to get out of ourselves, to get beyond our obstacles, is to find out what God wants us to learn in the process. What do I have to learn? It's difficult to learn anything about spiritual principles like faith, hope, and obedience while living on Easy Street, with everything going our way. As we confront the obstacles that arise from our own character defects (fear, lack of trust, anger, unforgiveness), as well as other hurdles that crop up in our paths, we have to continually ask, "What can I learn from Him in this process?"

We waste so much precious energy trying to manipulate or control God. That energy is so much better spent steering a course towards trust. The first step of trust is awareness. We have to be aware that we are nothing more, nothing less, than children of God.

Following Your Intellect Might be Bad Advice

We have to stop slotting God into intellectual categories. We have to give up, to stop pretending that our finite minds can control or even grasp the infinite. If we surrender ourselves instead, then faith can move in. Conversion can move in that process.

Conversion or metanoia takes place on two different levels - the head and the heart. Very often we get stuck in the head. Someone once said, "There's a long distance between the head and the heart." I remember hearing that and believing it, because very often, we have the knowledge. We have the knowledge on some level, but we just don't have the deep experience of that knowledge. We haven't yet embraced the fullness of the experience. So, conversion must take place in both the head and in the heart. We have to understand, again, that intimacy with God (or with a friend or loved one) must incorporate both the head and the heart.

Of course, neither faith nor trust in God robs us of our mental capacity. Sometimes people who think that religion is a crutch will look at Christians and say, "That is such a childlike way of looking at the world. God will help you or God will be there." But is it? Is it childlike or is it trusting in the God of creation?

Maybe we have lost some of that wonderful childlike trust; maybe we have become too guarded, even from ourselves. But the world doesn't understand that. Even if we live in the purest of Christian homes, there is still a worldly influence that imparts doubt on us. Because we were raised in the world, we have a tendency to struggle with "Oh, maybe I shouldn't trust as much," or "Maybe I should look at this and take a more intellectual approach to it." But in fact, we are called to have that faith, to have that deep level of trust that God is directing us.

He is not going to rob us of our natural ability to think. It's just not going to happen. It is really difficult for some to trust, because our human experiences and relationships often rob us. The only way we can learn to trust is if we stop worshiping our intellect, our flesh, and allow God's grace to move us in the Spirit.

No matter how enthusiastic or zealous, we all occasionally harbor doubts, fears, and lack of trust in God. This is only human. One of my favorite scripture passages is where Jesus is in the Garden of Gethsemane and He is literally sweating blood knowing the horror of the cross that awaits Him. What did Jesus do as these fears crept in? He knelt down and prayed to Abba. Jesus prayed, "Your will, Abba, not mine." I think there is something for us to learn from that.

1 Corinthians 12:36 *"No one can say that Jesus is Lord except under the influence of the Holy Spirit."*

Many can call Jesus their savior, their friend and even their brother...Jesus as Lord is another question. Oh I'm sure we

33

can all say the words, however, that's not what I mean. Jesus is Lord!! That means we are his subjects. That means He is our ALL. In our distrust, we don't allow Jesus to lord over all areas of our lives. We want to stay in control, but the paradox is even the word Lord means that He is in control— just like the Lord of the mansion.

If you think about it, we are mocking God when we pray, "Hallowed be Thy name, Thy kingdom come, Thy will be done"…if we harbor a secret agenda to promote our own will…. rather than the will of God.

I think sometimes we take on life - we trust in us - more than we trust in God. I hear people saying things like "I have to make sure that my kids are going to church every Sunday," or "I have to do this," and "I have to do that." Sometimes it's just a phrase that we use, but more often, we really believe it. We really believe that we are in control. If we would give up some of this stuff that we hold so precious, we would find that God is going to be God in the process. Of course, we need to give good example to our children and we are responsible for raising them according to God's law. Trusting in God doesn't mean that we don't have to concern ourselves; it means we don't have to worry.

The more we grow in our trust in God and the less we re-sist, the more we become like clay in the Potter's wheel, ready to be molded and created anew. The more I allow Him to transform me into the Gospel, the more those people that come into contact with me are going to be transformed by what they experience with me. So I need only concentrate on being the best servant of Christ that I can be, and relinquish my imagined control over other people, places, and things. Recognizing our own power-lessness is a big change for so many of us.

That's a leap for many of us because now I have to say, as far as my children are concerned, "God, You really do need to care for my kids." Not that I stand back and let everything happen, but I have to concentrate on being a good example and a good parent. I have to trust Him enough so that He transforms me. The solution is in putting effort into being the very best parent I can be in Christ, which means dying of self. It's only an egotistical illusion that we have the power to make our children into anything, except possibly neurotics if we harp on them all the time.

Trusting in God with our children means loving them, enjoying them and empowering them to be all they can be with the gifts God gave them. Too many parents, because they have felt unfulfilled in their own relationships or career choices, try to mold their kids into what they are not. We are not the potters; Abba is. The principal of powerlessness is the key to a serene life. I am powerless over my husband; all that need concern me is what kind of wife I am. I am powerless over my bosses; instead I need to concentrate only on what kind of worker I am. I am powerless over my neighbors but not over what kind of neighbor that I am.

I think about Jesus a lot. Take a look at the beginning of the Gospel of John, where it says, *"and the Word became flesh."* If we really look at that, what does it mean? Well, to me it means that everything He said, everything He did, and all of his attitudes were exactly what The Word was. There was no contradiction in what He did and what He said. I think that we, as believing Christians, have to allow God to change us to the point that we are saying, doing, acting, and behaving the Gospel. It's not enough to preach it; there are enough preachers out there. We must become it! That takes trust. He will bring us onto paths that allow us to be changed. These paths aren't always walks in the park. A hard road will always change us for the better if we take advantage of the grace that always comes with the yoke.

Let God Transform You

I teach at St. Vincent de Paul Regional Seminary where men prepare to become Catholic priests. I push my seminarians all the time, to look at and wrestle with their own issues, because when you are ministering to someone else it's not a good time to start looking at yourself. You need to reach the point where it's not about you anymore; it's about the other person. It has to be about the people to whom you minister. All of us have the opportunity to minister to others and we need to prepare ourselves for that.

So take this time now to let God transform us, so that when we look at others, we can only see God's beauty in him or her. We have to allow God to work on us so that when we speak the Gospel, when we preach it, we are it. God through His grace allows that to happen, but we have to trust Him. Transformation from the worrier to a servant of God can only happen if you trust Him.

I truly believe, in my heart of hearts, that God is asking each of us and is calling each of us to step out of the narrow confines into which we have unknowingly boxed ourselves. I believe that He is speaking to each one of us, telling us just how narrow are our confines and urging us to broaden ourselves. Yes, it's going to take an act of faith to be able to push those walls back. He is going to reveal things to us but He never directs us to do anything without giving us access to the strength and the power we need to carry out His will. Listen in your heart. Try not to be impatient, just listen. God will expose the narrow confines and together, you and He can work out a plan for stretching.

36

I believe that we are being asked to proclaim like St. Thomas, "Nothing but Thee," or like St. Theresa, "God alone." I know we say these things and we sing such incredibly beautiful worship songs. The words are so powerful, but do we really let them be a part of who we are? Or do we sing very beautiful songs, and then forget that those songs are really designed to change us?

Scripture is the Word of God, the Living Word of God. That means that every single time we hear a word from Scripture, it should be transforming us in some way. We should be changed in some way. It's the Living Word. It's not a good book. It's the Living Word. The Word goes in and it does something to us. If we are stopping it from doing that, if we're saying, "Look, I've had enough," then fear is talking ...not trust.

Psalm 27:1 *"The Lord is my Light and salvation; whom should I fear?"*

What are we afraid of? We're His kids. We're the King's kids. We're His babies. He's saying, "No, you don't stop growing until I call you home." Remember, His desire for us is abundant life. But we need to trust.

We're faced with dealing with trust on two levels: with our hearts and with our minds. Not only do we have to make the intellectual decision to trust God, but we also have to accomplish this wholeheartedly. Our hearts, knowing that we are truly children of God, embrace His will and grace. That egocentric part of ourselves, which can be very devout, tends to relate God's will to our own preferences. You know, "I don't feel good, God, change me." "This is uncomfortable. I don't want to have this anymore." We need to be aware of this egocentric side of us. We need to look at our egos. This doesn't mean we aren't lovers of God if we have it, but the more it decreases and the more we allow that true child of God to emerge, we find new life.

We learn to not be so emotionally invested in our preferred outcomes, in our will. We learn something about acceptance, accepting God's plan and God's will for our lives.

Acquiring an attitude of trust and acceptance changes everything. Do you know that feeling you get if you wear a new dress or a new suit? Attitude is a million times deeper than that. It changes our whole outlook....which means it changes everything we see.

Having an attitude of trust in God means that, instead of experiencing fear at the inevitable bumps in the road, we embrace life's trials with a peace that surpasses all human understanding. These are not empty words or promises, this is God's truth. It doesn't mean that we become oblivious to the world around us, it means we start to view it through a different lens. A lens that allows us to more clearly see the path that connects us with Jesus the Victor rather than with a lens that only allows us to see the immediate problem or the suffering. With trust and acceptance, we know that we are children of God and have not been abandoned.

Jesus constantly taught his apostles to trust even though He also told them fearful things. He told them about his impending death. "I'm going to be crucified. Trust." He gave them the reality of what they needed to be doing. "Trust me through everything!" - not just the good days, not just the moments that are okay, or the moments that we are praising and worshipping and everything is all in order. No, he said, "Trust me through everything!" Everything!

The trust to which He called people wasn't based on the denial of the reality of suffering and evil. The cross was real. We can't get to the glory unless we go through that cross. He didn't! Why should we think it is going to be any different for us? But if we hold on, if we trust, we get through it. I don't know about you, but everything really worthwhile that I have learned on the journey, every cross that I have had to bear, has been designed to temper me…to make me stronger, better, happier, more joyous and free.

Proverb 3:5 *Trust in the LORD with all your heart, on your own intelligence rely not;*

Silly Defenses…Unless They're Ours

As we journey and risk dying of self, we are forced to look beyond our defense mechanisms. We are very good at protecting our psyche. Defense mechanisms sometimes deny: "I never sin." They rationalize: "My sins are definitely not as bad as others," or " God knows why I won't forgive my husband and it's OK with Him." Defense mechanisms protect: "That person is so into himself and not like me." Sometimes they displace, pushing our own emotions off on someone else: "I have to teach this dog a lesson he will never forget."

We need to become more aware of these defense mechanisms that become like walls, because they block us from the Holy Spirit. We have to be tough with ourselves. All defense mechanisms are not immediately bad. Some are even good for short-term coping, especially when we are young. We don't need defense mechanism to protect ourselves when we have the King of Kings to protect us.

At some point, if we truly want to be free, we have to take the risk. We have to say, "In You Lord I will not be afraid. Come into my heart and help me look at that baggage that has been keeping me captive. I want to know where my sinfulness is coming from and I want to take responsibility for it." As Henry Nouwen says, "The more we know that we are God's Beloved, the easier it becomes to risk. "

Psalm 143:10 - *Teach me to do Your will, for You are my God. May Your good spirit lead me on level ground.*

"Teach me to do Your will." God teaches us, but sometimes when we see the plan, one of our defense mechanisms kicks in and then we forget or reject His plan. How many have been called to stop smoking? We know that we need to stop, and so many of my patients do quit, but then temptation comes and our minds rationalize: "I'll just smoke for a short while to stay calm, I know now that I can stop whenever I want to." No!!! The plan was to stop--- God's will for your life is to have a healthy body. We slip back into old familiar beliefs. He's saying, " You're asking me to teach you and I'm going to teach you. I want to bring you to that level ground." Level ground - very often, we're not on level ground. He wants to bring us there.

In fairness to smokers, we all rationalize. Who among us has never procrastinated or become complacent when God put it on our hearts to do something?

We need to ask ourselves some questions. Do I trust enough to see the good in each day? Do I trust The Lord even when my plan is being shot down and the alternative is not as appealing to me? Do I really trust enough to risk not being accepted by others? Am I willing to stand up for Christ? In all environments, am I willing to stand up for you, Lord? Do I trust that You are real and that You love me? I think that is one of the greatest questions. Do I really, really believe that God is in love with me? I know I say it, and I even tell other people that God loves them, but do I really, really believe it for myself? Do I love myself the way You love me? Have I failed to be a vessel of blessings because of my fears or concerns?

These are all trust issues. What gets in the way of me trusting You? Have I blocked being drawn into the silence of my soul for fear I may hear Your voice? A lot of people are afraid to sit quietly. Very often, I'll hear people say things like, "You know, when I'm busy, I'm fine. I can be busy and get things done but when it's time to sit quietly, then I get very anxious." Well, sure, you're alone with yourself and with your God. We have to learn how to be comfortable with that.

I prayed with a pastor once, the pastor of a small non-denominational church, and he said, "You know, Catholics are so fortunate because they have always had that quiet time. They can sit before the Blessed Sacrament and be quiet. They know how to do that." He went on to say, "When I try to teach my congregation, they don't understand. They don't understand how to be quiet." That's when God speaks to our soul - when we sit quietly before Him. But people put up walls and blocks and barricades, because they don't trust what they're going to hear. They don't trust the living God.

We need to ask ourselves, "Am I really sharing the precious gifts that God has given me with other people?" I have to believe that I am worthy of gifts. I have to believe that I have gifts. One of the toughest questions for people to answer when

41

they come into counseling or spiritual direction is "What are your gifts?"

Patients tend to answer, "Oh, I don't know. I don't think I have any." Well then, the Scripture is wrong. Then God is a liar. "I don't have any?" How could that be? I have them. If I have gifts, you have to have gifts - because we're all the same. Nobody's different. We're all the same. God gifted all of us. Either God lying or you are, and I'm going to bet my bottom dollar that God's not lying. So what are your gifts? We need to know our gifts and we need to be sharing them with other people.

Our Lord is calling us to a journey in trust, because He has so many greater things in store for us, but we settle for crumbs, measly crumbs. He has the whole cake in front of us, but we take the crumbs. We have to trust Him.

Matthew 11:28-30 – *"Come to me, all you who are weary and burdened, and I will give you rest. Take my yoke upon you and learn from me for I am gentle and humble in heart and you will find rest for your soul, for my yoke is easy and my burden is light."*

God is clearly telling us He is gentle and humble. Yet so many people still hold on to a God who is a tyrant, who is the authoritarian, and who is going to throw us into the fiery abyss. We rationalize, "If I do this, He'll get me. If I don't do this right, then He will punish me." But He doesn't say that. He says He is gentle and humble of heart. Look at His actions. He chose to be a humble carpenter, born in a manger with poor parents. This is a God who loves us so much that He is willing to lay His life down for us. He's not a liar. He speaks truth!

Psalm 118:8-9 – *"It is better to take refuge in the Lord than to trust in man. It is better to take refuge in the Lord than to trust in princes."*

We need to continue to examine trust. Trust is really the fiber that runs through all of the blocks. We want to reach that point when we can surrender and say, "Lord, no matter what the cost, I trust you."

I remember a mother who lived in Canada. Her daughter was in a head-on collision with a truck. They didn't know if she was going to make it through the night. The 17-year-old girl did actually make it through the night, but she was still in kind of a coma state. The nurses said that the next few hours would tell what would happen with this young woman. Distraught, her mother sought refuge in a church. She happened to arrive in time for a noon weekday mass. Just as the mom went up to receive the Eucharist, just as she was walking up, she realized in her heart of hearts that she had really given up her daughter to the Lord. She then spoke the words, "Lord, she's yours. You love her more than I do and Your will be done."

After mass, the mother went back to the hospital, and when she got there, the nurses immediately ran over. Her heart just sank at that point because they stopped her from going into the room. The nurse said, "I didn't want you to be alarmed. Something happened about twenty minutes ago. We don't know what it was, but your daughter is sitting up and eating pizza." You know, our God is such a wonderful God. He's so good!

We get back grace from God in proportion to the amount of trust we place with Him. It's a spiritual paradox that the only way to win is to surrender. The tough part, the challenge for all of us, is that God demands an unconditional surrender.

How many of us try to negotiate the terms of our surrender with half measures or by muttering, "OK, God do this for me and I will do that for you." Put down the rifles. Trust in the Lord with your whole heart. Be not afraid. And whatever you do, don't be half baked, half hearted, or take half measures!

Exercises For Trust

- <u>Start slowly.</u> Trust takes time to grow. A good beginning is the awareness that change and growth take time.

- <u>Recognize</u> who or what in your lifetime has gained your trust. Read 2 Chronicles 20 *"Trust in the Lord your God and you will be found firm."* Are you trusting in your bank account, in your worry, in your spouse, or in the God of creation?

- <u>Listen</u> to your self-talk. Ask yourself whether it's based on truth...or lies. For example, on some level do you believe lies like: *"God only loves good people."* Read John 3:16. *"God so loved the world that He gave His only Son that whoever believes in Him may not die but have eternal life."* Don't live in the future. Don't live in absolutes. Don't live in lies.

- <u>Read</u> one chapter per day of the New Testament.

- <u>Start a faith journal</u>. Make the following journal entries.

    1. Who in my life do I trust?
    2. Why?
    3. When have I trusted people most?
    4. Has there been an event (or events) that has weakened my trust in others?
    5. When have I trusted God most?
    6. Has their been an event that has weakened my trust in God?
    7. Has there been a time that has strengthened my trust with others?
    8. Has there been a time that has strengthened my trust and Faith in the Lord? (clue: God hasn't changed, what's changed about you?)

Chapter 4

Mind Traps

Romans 12:2 *"Do not conform yourself to this age, but be transformed by the renewal of your mind so that you may judge what is God's will, what is good, pleasing, and perfect"*

Before we get into this chapter, I want to invite each of you to start thinking in terms of truth and lies. At the end of this chapter, it is my hope that you will be prepared to answer these two questions:

- "What kind of lies about myself, have I been told, that I have come to believe to be true?

- "What kind of lies about myself, have I learned to tell myself, that I have come to believe to be true?"

The following story, briefly mentioned in the second chapter, bears repeating in a little more detail because it so clearly demonstrates how lies can become our reality.

I was asked to minister to a beautiful teenaged girl. She was gorgeous. The family thought she was mentally ill, or at least neurotic, because she refused to go out in public without covering her entire face with a scarf or floppy hat. Ten minutes into my first meeting with her, I realized that she had spent a lifetime with a mother who called her "God-awful ugly" at least ten times each day. The poor girl's mind started to believe the lie and then acted upon it by covering her angelic face. The lie of "God-awful ugly" had become her truth. In reality, she is beautiful.

The single most common lie I hear in my practice from Christians is, "I am worthless." If this is your truth, then you believe something like this: "He can't use me. I'm not good enough for the Kingdom. God messed up and made a mistake when He created me. God has no plans for me, I am worthless and so why even try."

You can't imagine how often I see patients who tell themselves this lie. The lie has a payoff. Many rationalize and conveniently get themselves off the hook of doing God's will, or working on any sort of spiritual program other than maybe weekly church attendance, by saying to themselves, "Oh, God really can't use me. I have no special gifts or talents."

Here's another one people tell themselves: "If God really loved me, I wouldn't suffer so much hurt and pain. Life should be easier for poor me." Sometimes there is a sad twist: "I must really be sinful because God won't help me. I feel so unworthy and guilty; God must really be unhappy with me. No matter how hard I try, it's not good enough for God."

So many Christians have nurtured these false beliefs from childhood. Belief systems that do not come from God are lies. If you are wondering if it's truth or a lie, hold it up to the Word. Hold it up to the Light.

Some lies really sound like truth, and very often, when I start to work with these people in spiritual direction or in psychological counseling, it's tough to break through that wall. When I try to challenge the distorted belief, they will usually respond in validation to the lie, "No, no, it is truth."

What's truth about it? Again, can you hold it up to God's Word? I don't remember seeing in the Bible that some of us are worthless. Scripture tells us in Isaiah that we are precious, all of us! No one is eliminated. He has called us all by name. It's ridiculous to think He has called everyone but you! He loves us all unconditionally. He is our Abba. If you can't hold it up to God's word, then it's not right. It's not truth.

A college student I taught was told while she was a teenager, "You will never graduate from high school." Guess what? She didn't graduate high school. She lived up to the expectation of her parents. Well, when I met her, she said she always thought she was stupid. She used to say to herself, "I can't do anything. I didn't graduate high school. I could certainly never go to college." But, in fact, when she was in her thirties, she got her GED and I was her professor in her last class in college. She had a 4.0 grade point average. She said, "It took until I was 36 or 37 to realize that in fact I could do it and I could have done it then."

She believed the lie. She believed herself stupid. Her mind told her that she couldn't do it. She couldn't make anything of herself and she spent years believing that and living it. How many people tell themselves they're too fat, they're too skinny, they're too ugly, they're not lovable. People do this all the time!

I have a sister who is twelve years older than me. My parents had just the two of us and, with the great age difference, we were almost raised like only children.

I had wonderful parents. They didn't always do everything right, but none of us do. One thing I remember hearing from my aunt when I was little was, "When your sister was born, she was beautiful. Oh, she had this curly strawberry blonde hair and milk-white skin." Then she said, "When you were born, you scared everyone." Wow, I thought. "You scared everyone!" Sometimes my older cousins would get into it, "Oh, when we saw you, you scared us. You were so skinny and you had that black hair all over you!" Ouch! Thank you very much!

I would hear that and later I would hear things like, "But now you're attractive." But it was too little too late and didn't fix the hurt or my self esteem issues. It didn't heal me completely. Praise God, healing came, but slowly. It started when my husband came into my life, when we were sixteen. We were childhood sweethearts and he looked at me differently. He would look at me in a way that I would feel very beautiful. God planted him right there. But even that didn't completely heal the lies about me being so ugly. I didn't start living completely in the truth until our youngest son was born. He is the stamp of me. He was so cute and I could see myself in him and, for the first time in my life, see the truth of what I look like.

Look how long it took before God brought that healing to fullness. It was in my mind. I believed it. No one really ever came out and flat said, "You are ugly". But from early on that's what I believed.

We put memories, thoughts, and interpretations together as if they are so many pieces of a jigsaw puzzle. All too often, we put the pieces together incorrectly into a false image and then we embrace that.

50

We believe what we have embraced and we hold onto a picture that isn't truth. If we don't ever get to the point of unraveling the lies, we remain in the prison of those distorted memories and beliefs. We stay stuck!

Remember the scripture quote that we used to open this chapter. *"Do not conform yourself to this age, but be transformed by the renewal of your mind so that you may judge what is God's will, what is good, pleasing, and perfect."*

What is good? It's so easy to rationalize "good." It often becomes something that is unattainable. Then our minds jump to the conclusion that " I'm never good enough, I can never hit the mark, and furthermore I don't even know what the mark is." Then, to add insult to injury, we project our perceptions of ourselves onto others and onto God. I start to see myself as not good enough and think every one else around me knows that I'm not good enough, including God. It becomes truth for us. We can distort scripture interpretations to support the lies we believe.

People-Pleasers

What is pleasing? We know what people-pleasers are like: "If I can please you then you will know that I'm really a good person. I can feel better about myself if you feel good about me."

There are a lot of people-pleasers in life. The world promotes this view. We have been raised in a culture that tells us that a school report card of "A" means great, "B" not as great, and "C" is average. We translate that to mean if I get an "A" I am wonderful, "B" not so wonderful, and with "C" or below I must be a loser.

Think of all the stuff your mind has been exposed to along the way. "You are a bad girl because you got your clothes dirty." Does this mean that all of me is bad just because of one stupid mud pie?

Therefore, in our minds, "pleasing" tends to become anything others see and express as pleasing. Who I am is directly connected to what is pleasing to you. People pleasers go through life trying to please others, not necessarily by giving people what they need or want, but what the pleaser imagines that they need or want. Of course, people pleasers often get rejected and the nasty cycle is that this rejection then tends to fulfill their own vision of themselves.

We transfer beliefs about our self onto the heart of God. We try to please God so that He will see us as pleasing. However, trying harder doesn't make it happen because it's our vision of ourselves, not His. For example, individuals have shared with me how saying their prayer just the right way, with just the right words, are the only prayers that are pleasing to God.

I had a patient; I'll call her Michelle. Her mother had frequently told her that God would never listen to her prayers because Michelle was so displeasing to God. The girl believed her mom. Michelle grew up to truly believe that God would have nothing to do with her. From this example, perhaps you can more clearly see how things in our mind can block the grace of God. In Michelle's mind, the blockage was so severe that even her prayers couldn't reach God. So of course, she long ago stopped praying.

Other people act pious in a certain way, out of the mistaken belief that only in this way will they be pleasing to God! When really, the only thing that God wants is our heart. He doesn't care how we do it. He just wants our heart. We can't do it perfectly. His love for us is not based on what we do or don't do. He loves us unconditionally. He wants to be our All in All and we miss the point because of the little or big lies that get in the way. When our mind isn't healed, when our mind isn't whole, when we haven't uncovered the lies, it becomes very difficult to know God's love for us.

Perfectionism

Perfectionism is a common block. Scripture tells us *"what is perfect, what is perfect."* Well, that is one of the most dangerous words. I remember one patient who was obsessed with perfection. He would demand certain perfection of his wife and to justify his perfectionism he would say, "This is the way God wants it. He calls us to be perfect, and this is what perfect is." He would bring me a list of Scriptures about perfection. The problem was he always put his spin on perfection and missed the true meaning of what God is calling us to. To be perfect like our heavenly Father really means that we need to strive for unconditional and complete love like our heavenly Father has for us. God really doesn't care if you clean your home so that it shines brighter than the neighbors or that your children are always impeccably dressed. He cares most about the way we love.

Perfection doesn't come from what we do. It's not the destination of our spiritual journey. Rather, we have to recognize that perfectionism slows me down, prevents me from moving forward. To back off from perfectionist thoughts, attitudes and behaviors takes trust. Remember that T word (trust), we'll hear it often because it makes up the foundation of all the barriers to healing.

We have to release things and release people. When we look at people and say, "Aw, they're really not doing it the right way," then we need to back off. We need to say, "God, You deal with them." There are no perfect humans and to continue to embrace the lie of perfectionism means that I deny that I am human. We must accept and embrace our humanism. God created us as humans, not gods.

I heard something really wonderful from a friend recently who says he is recovering from perfectionism. As the father of three, through the years, he had gotten into the habit of telling his wife and children to do this or to do that in exactly such and such a way. Very opinionated about everything, my friend realized that he was making his family miserable as he suffered under the delusion, "Everything will be perfect just as long as everyone does things exactly like I direct them."

The way he broke himself of this lie was by adopting an attitude of "no comment." If his daughter wore certain shoes he didn't like or his wife didn't spice dinner exactly to perfection, instead of commenting as usual, he would bite his tongue and whisper to himself, "no comment." "I was amazed", he said later, "maybe a hundred times those first couple of days I shut my trap and didn't comment. Guess what, without my attention into everyone else's business, things got better!"

Looking at the Person in the Mirror

Charles Solomon, in his book Handbook to Happiness, states, "Most believers live with an identity that has been assigned to them, either positive or negative, depending on the extent of rejection, or with an identity that has been built for them."

At infancy, we're all natural. We are who we are. Then as we start to grow, different rules and regulations are placed on us. All of the sudden, that natural part of us is squashed. We become what we think we should become, depending on how we were raised, depending on the teachers that we had, depending on the neighbors and friends and what they saw in us. That's the way we build our identity.

You might have a C student or a D student that's trying as hard as he or she can. Perhaps that's all he or she can get, compared with an A student that is sailing through life. But yet, that D student is looked at in a certain way. Their self-esteem gets damaged early and forty years later they end up in my office telling me how worthless they are and how miserable their lives are. We have to find ways to encourage people rather than to condemn them in their experience.

A theorist, appropriately named Cooley, constructed something called Cooley's Looking Glass Self. The theory is simply that you see your reflection in other people, in their reaction to you or attitude toward you. You live up to their reflection and then you become what they reflect to you. It's like self-fulfilling prophecy in that you take ownership of a lie, and make it your truth.

Therefore if my parents see me in a certain way, and maybe that's not a very good way, then I'm going to start to see myself that way and I'm going to start to behave that way. That's the stuff that has to be healed, because it becomes so much a part of us that we can't separate it from the truth. We don't see the difference. So many of us are living in an identity that has been conformed to this world. Our identities need to be transformed by the power of God. Remember my student, "you'll never graduate high school," - she didn't. "You are God-awful ugly." - She wasn't.

Positive words are even more empowering and we need to use them more. We need to use them not only on our children and others but on ourselves as well. The Isaiah Scriptures are so wonderful for building up the truth of who we are. Isaiah 49:5 says, "I am made glorious in the sight of the Lord and my God is my strength". Verse 49:16 says," See, upon the palms of my hands I have written your name....I will never forget you" WOW!

1 Timothy - *For God has <u>not</u> given us a spirit of fear, but of power and of love and of a sound mind.*

We can't just look over these Scriptures and let them pass and then live the same lies anymore. He has already given us a sound mind. Whenever we cannot hold something up to Scripture, get rid of it. Trust that the Lord will put it in order for you. We don't need to hold on to those old beliefs about ourselves, those lies. Most of the time, they're condemning.

Solutions

There are solutions and we'll go through some of them. We need to know where our identity came from. We need to know why we look at ourselves the way we do. We need to put aside self-criticism, check the condemnation at the door, and dispassionately zoom out and look back at our lives.

Whatever we find, we can't play the blame game. Forgiveness is crucial and there will be a whole chapter on that. I don't think we should condemn our parents or people from the past. Everybody does the best that they can. There are very few people, and I've never met any, who are out there just to hurt us because they want to hurt us. They have their own blocks and their own lies. We need only to look at ourselves, how we have been formed, our identity, and the lies we tell ourselves.

We need to recognize that the other people in our lives aren't perfect and they do make mistakes. We also make mistakes and we need to work on acceptance, concentrating only on changing the things we can.

Bill Wilson, the founder of Alcoholics Anonymous, wrote "It is a spiritual axiom that whenever something is wrong...then there is something wrong with us." What he means by this is that when we are troubled, upset, angry, or fearful.... those are things going on inside of me. It's me that's become angry and fearful. If I am fearful or angry.... then I have a problem. The theory is that as long as I am being the best parent I can be, the best spouse I can be, the best employee I can be.... then I don't have to fall off the spiritual beam just because my boss did this, my child did that, or my spouse made some sort of mistake.

Our happiness and serenity need not be contingent upon what the boss feels like today or whether my neighbor smiled at me this morning. Our state of grace need not be affected by what the weather is doing today nor whether traffic is heavy or light.

Tom, a dentist friend of mine, likes to conjure up images of whirling dervishes. We all have whirling dervishes dancing through our lives. Sometimes they whirl harmlessly by, and sometimes they upset the furniture around us. We drive ourselves nuts if we try to concentrate on changing them, when all we can really hope to change is ourselves. As Tom likes to say, "Let 'em whirl."

Consider the Serenity Prayer:

God grant me the serenity to accept the things I cannot change,
The courage to change the things that I can,
And the wisdom to know the difference.

The bottom line is that the only possible thing we can change is ourselves. It's only an illusion that we have the power to change the boss, the neighbor, or our spouses. If we are upset, if we have a problem, then 99 times out of a hundred the thing we need to change is ourselves. We have to want to change. Sometimes, as mature Christians, we don't want to change anymore. We did it. You know, been there, done that, and I don't want to change anymore. That's a lie. God calls us to have that desire to change and progress throughout our lives.

We cannot self-condemn. Promise yourself and promise God that you will not condemn yourself. That doesn't mean we don't repent. It means that instead of staying stuck in our failures, we learn from them and move on. We are reflections of the Light. I see too many lights that are covered with such heavy baggage; you can't even tell that they are lights.

Self-condemnation is not of the Lord. It doesn't allow us to draw people to the Lord. Instead, it makes people question, "What's so great about being a Christian? This person's not happy and that person's not going through that particular trial in life with such great strides. What's so good about Christianity?" We are called to be the light, so we have to stop beating ourselves up and condemning ourselves. We need to look at our shortcomings, turn them over to the care of God, learn from it, grow, and move on.

Look at your accomplishments through God's eyes. We've done a lot and we need to look and allow God to show us our progress, because our gifts are going to be there. Our talents are going to be there. I think we were taught early on that if you see your gifts, if you see your accomplishments, then you're conceited. We used to hear that word all the time. "Oh, you're conceited." But in reality, He's gifted us. We didn't do it. He gave us our gifts.

If someone were to give me a brand new car, I'd go around saying, "Hey, did you see my wonderful brand new red sports car? Paul gave it to me." I'd be telling everybody, right? Well, we need to do the same thing with God. "Hey, hear my wonderful voice and how wonderfully I play that guitar and lead worship? God gave me that!" That is something to be proud of! He gave it to us and we need to appreciate it and talk about it. Let's tell people about our gifts and go out of our way to recognize each other's giftedness.

Attitude is Everything

There's no room - and this is really important - there's no room in spiritual abundance for being negative toward others or ourselves. Negativity keeps us stuck. It keeps our minds stuck, whether it is in self-condemnation or in picking out everything that is wrong with everybody else.

"Well, this person doesn't sit right, doesn't walk right, doesn't talk right, doesn't do this right, and doesn't do that right." Or, "See that person out there, look at her." We need to stop being critical because that is not the way God corrects us

We need to be particularly careful about criticizing our children. The other day, in a supermarket checkout line, I heard a mother say in a very condemning and loud voice, "Stop crying you sissy." The child was only about four and had just fallen.

Our self-esteem is very, very fragile no matter how well we seem to hide it. The world would be so much better if we spent the energy empowering one another rather than criticizing. Don't fall into the trap of expecting empowerment from others; concentrate instead on being an empower-giver instead of taker. Encourage, rather than drag down.

Prayer of St. Francis

Lord,
Make me an instrument of Your peace;
Where there is hatred let me sow love;
Where there is injury, pardon;
Where there is doubt, faith;
Where there is despair, hope;
Where there is darkness, light;
And where there is sadness, joy.

O divine Master,
Grant that I may not so much seek
To be consoled as to console,
To be understood as to understand,
To be loved as to love,
For it is in giving that we receive,
It is in pardoning that we are pardoned
And it is in dying that we are born
To eternal life.

Whatever we give comes back to us in the form of grace. This is what the beautiful prayer of St. Francis is all about.

Let's look for the gifts in one another and share them so that I hear mine through you and you hear yours through me. We need to do that for one another.

His word is truth. His personality is love. We need to be enmeshed in God's word. It needs to be so much a part of us that we can recognize lies. We need to be so in touch with scripture that when the old thoughts come back, we immediately know this is not from God. So rather than reading the Scriptures and studying them just with that head knowledge, we have to digest it in a new way where we can begin to appreciate and recognize truth. It's like developing a built-in lie detector.

We have to be open to what God can do. We have to look into His mirror. Not the mirror that we've been looking into all along - but His mirror - so that He reflects back to us the truth of what He sees in us. We need to look into the mirror and see ourselves as His beloved children. Anything else we see is just a lie created by our minds.

Here's those two questions that you might want to take a minute and ask yourself now:

- "What kind of lies about myself, have I been told, that I have come to believe to be true?
- "What kind of lies about myself, have I learned to tell myself, that I have come to believe to be true?"

 Chapter 5

Armored Hearts

Psalm 147:3 – *"He heals the broken-hearted, binding up their wounds"*

The last chapter focused on the mind. This chapter delves into matters of the heart and next will discuss the role of body in blocking grace. Of course, please remember that these are all interconnected. After reading anecdotes like "God-awful ugly", I hope that you can clearly see how your mind can trick you into believing lies and how these lies can cause you to hide from the nourishment of God's healing grace. Inappropriate ways of dealing with heartache can similarly block us. Ironically mishandling heartache can block us from the very grace we need to heal a broken heart.

If we believe that He heals the broken-hearted, then we have to take another step out of our brokenness. Sometimes we are not even conscious of the brokenness in our hearts but we need to allow God to reveal and open up those areas that might unconsciously be causing a block.

When we've had any kind of spiritual or emotional hurt, we generally start to back away from relationships because we don't want to get hurt again. When we back away from other people, we also tend to back away from God. This is important, so let me repeat it: **When we experience hurt, we consciously or unconsciously tend to back away from God, the only One who can truly heal us.**

Anything that happens in our relationship with others also happens in our relationship with God. Often, my patients will say, "My relationship with God is just wonderful but I just don't really like some people." Many people believe that they can hate people (like ex-spouses) and simultaneously be in wonderful communion with God. What happens when we hold this idea up to scripture? Can anyone find the place where it says, "Love God and hate your neighbors?" No, I don't think so.

Hurt manifests itself in different ways. We may not even realize that our hurts certainly affect our relationship with God and with those around us. Instead of opening our hearts to the Lord, so many of us instead start bullet-proofing our hearts by erecting shields, barricades, blocks, and all sorts of obstacles that keep us from His healing grace.

1 Chronicles 28:9 – *"Know the God of your father and serve Him with a whole heart and a willing mind."*

We don't serve God with a whole heart when we are building barriers and distancing ourselves from people and from God. We don't have a whole heart when our heart is still broken and damaged. We don't have that whole heart to give Him, and often we don't even realize our own brokenness.

A number of years ago, I was heading for a retreat with the Association for Christian Therapists. I was flying over to the west coast of Florida. It's a wonderful three-day retreat and conference. I told myself on the way over, and this is such a pious statement, "Lord -if you need me to pray for anyone while

I'm there, please just reveal them to me and I will certainly pray for them." Isn't that pious?

At my first Mass there, as the priest elevated the Host, God put on my heart that I was going to pray with the priest. So the first thing I thought was, "Oh, the poor thing, he needs me to pray with him." But I didn't see him again until Mass the next day.

The next morning, as he elevated the Host again, God gave me a picture of my heart. It was a flesh heart that was covered very tightly in saran wrap! I had a vision of my heart wrapped tightly in plastic wrap.

It was then I knew that I wasn't going to be praying for this priest, but that he was going to be praying for me. Up until that point, I didn't know anything was wrong, except that I didn't love in the same way as before. After some prayer and reflection, I realized that I was telling myself a lie. I had told myself, "Well, I guess as you get older, you don't love the same; you don't love with the same intensity anymore. This probably happens to everyone." I believed it because I didn't have that same passion I had always had for people.

After mass, I asked the priest, Father Paul, to pray for me. He said, "Certainly. Give me a chance to get my vestments off and I will." The minute he sat down with me, he looked in my eyes and said, "Do you know you have your Father's eyes?" Well, the floodgates opened. There was a song at that time, Amy Grant's song **My Father's Eyes**, about how we are all made in His image and likeness. The song is about how we see good where most people don't.

I'm a trained therapist, but I couldn't stop crying, God was healing me.

The Lord gave this priest a picture of what had been going on in my life. I had experienced a series of painful rejections from people who were very close to me. Because of the hurt, I wasn't allowing myself to love in some way. I had become guarded. I was subconsciously protecting my heart from further damage and distancing myself from people and from God. Of course, I didn't realize it until it was over, but God did and brought me healing through this priest.

Upon my return from the conference, my husband Paul picked me up from the airport. I ran and grabbed him and said, "I am so sorry." He said, "Why?" He couldn't imagine what I had done. I said, "I haven't loved you the way I used to love you." He said, "You haven't?" He was unaware of my block but we were able to talk about it. It was only after God revealed my shielding Saran Wrap that I realized that I was not loving my husband nor my God in complete fullness.

<u>Serving God with a whole heart always means taking risk, becoming vulnerable to God's will for our lives</u>. If we want to be truly happy, then we need to become vulnerable. It means taking a chance and prayerfully looking deep inside ourselves and seeing what's there. No matter what He shows us, no matter what it is, He is revealing it so as to heal us. He's not showing it to us so that we'll be held prisoner in any way. He's showing it so that we can be freed.

Fear or Faith? It's Your Choice

Very often people believe that their fears are their security. "If I worry about this and work all the angles, then I'm safe, then I'm secure." Actually our fears and anxieties become our prisons. So we want to allow God to uncover these fears.

John 14:1 – *"Let not your heart be troubled; believe in God; believe also in me"*.

After a lifetime of stuffing our feelings, opening up and examining our secret fears is not easy. So many of us feel that it's like a Pandora's box inside where we have these fears safely contained. We falsely imagine that if we go in and open up the lid, then the vile stuff within is going to fly out and mess up all areas of our life. This image could not be farther from the truth. Remember, holding these hurts inside tends to increase our distance to the Lord and to the people we love. The only way we can be set free is to open up to the healing Light of the Lord.

It takes trusting (there is that "T" word again). I pray that if He hasn't started to open yours yet, that you will take the risk to open up your Pandora's box in the sight of the Lord. We need to put down our rifles and take a chance, even if we feel vulnerable and naked before the Lord. We need to unveil ourselves, to uncover the hurt, so we can see what's broken and allow Him to fix us.

We need to look at our fears. What are my fears of becoming totally intimate with Him and allowing intimacy with others? There are several fears that consciously or unconsciously tend to prevent us from experiencing intimacy:

> • **Merger** – Think of this in our relationship with the Lord. Some people fear losing control to God or to others...so they back off from intimacy and erect barriers to protect themselves from merger. "Lord, if I allow myself to be vulnerable to You, then You might control me."

67

• **Abandonment** – "You might leave me. So I just don't want to trust you totally, because then you may leave. This distrust is common and manifests itself in a variety of ways that prevent intimacy. I won't let you near my heart, because if you abandon me, it will hurt too much."

• **Exposure** - Sometimes we fear exposing who we really are to others and we live life as if we are hiding under a mask. " If you really knew how dirty and bad I am inside, then you wouldn't love me. So I will keep you from getting too close to my heart, so you don't find out the real me."

• **Attack** - We are afraid of lowering our shields for fear that we will come under attack just when we are most vulnerable. "If I let you in, then you will know my weaknesses and use them against me to hurt me in some way. If you know everything there is to know about me, you'll hurt me with your words or with your actions. No way am I going to lower my shields, I might come under attack."

• **Self-Destruction** – I am afraid that I will impulsively say something so stupid that it will hurt you. I won't tell you how I feel, or about my likes or dislikes, out of fear that you won't like me. This is a destructive impulse to lie to protect myself and keep others away from the real me.

All of these fears stop us from being intimate with one another and intimate with God. We have to lower the shields enough to let God in to fix our vulnerable hearts that we protect with fear.

How do we start or continue this journey of heart healing? We need to face our fears head on.

There is a fairy tale called Billy Goat Gruff. A mean old troll who lived under a bridge would try to scare away people from crossing it. The Lord always gives me a vision of this little troll whenever fear or concern or something gets in the way of going over that bridge towards greater intimacy with God and other people. Yes, there is a wretched little troll, and his name is fear, but he can't hurt me without my permission. We need to get over to the other side and the only way to do this is to face our fears.

People go to great lengths to avoid facing their fears. Maybe a lot of us can identify with Den's daughter Juliet. In the first grade, she was painfully shy and would have done anything to avoid making her first presentation in front of the entire class. Her fear of public speaking was so strong that she even asked her dad if they could move to another town. Instead, she and Den had a long talk about identifying fears, talking about them with someone you trust, and then facing them head on. Of course, no one in the class threw rocks at her, the presentation went beautifully, and Juliet experienced the euphoria and sense of personal triumph that comes when one identifies and faces their fears. Wasn't facing fear a whole lot easier than running away to another city and changing schools?

Fear is just a wretched old troll. When we are mustering the strength to stand up to fear, we can remember 1 John 4:18, *"Perfect love casts out all fear."* We already have the perfect love in Christ Jesus. We don't even have that far to go. We just have take a step out from under our umbrella to receive the grace. Fear is just a wretched little troll. We don't have to fear him. He can't hurt us.

Heart fear is different from *mind* fear. Mind fear is worry and anxiety. Heart fear manifests more in the hidden core belief that, "I am unlovable."

Fear is an enemy. It keeps us stuck. That's why God says, "Perfect love casts out all fear." He's not going to cast out something that is good. He's going to cast out that which keeps us paralyzed. It's fear that keeps wonderful Christian people paralyzed! We need to get rid of the fear. So many of us have become intimate with fear, rather than intimate with God. If you find yourself embracing fear, tell yourself, "I'm choosing to be intimate with fear instead of with God." He created us with free will and it's up to us whether we choose faith or fear. You can't have both.

In 2 Corinthians, St. Paul writes about how God spoke to his heart, *"My grace is sufficient for you, for power is perfected in weakness."* Just because we're not feeling strong doesn't mean we're not strong-hearted or that we can't tap into the power of the Lord. We need to embrace and believe. It is not always easy, but that's okay.

Trust that your triumph over adversity, heartache, and fear are part of God's plan for molding you into the person He wants you to be. Not unlike the story of little Juliet, the greatest triumphs and periods of growth and strengthening in my own adult life have resulted from facing adversity and fear with God at my side. (No matter how much the little girl in me was tempted to run)

Cardio-Resuscitation - Actions and Solutions for the Heart

- We need to be obedient to God's Word. We need to ask, "What does God's Word mean for me in my life?" Whatever that is, we need to be obedient to it. Meditate on what it means to obey God. God's will for us is to be peaceful, joyous and free.

- Don't repay injury with injury. Because, no matter how you rationalize it, if you act hurtful and negative towards someone, then you are well on your way to becoming a negative and hurtful person.

- Give forgiveness to those who have hurt you. Pray for them and their needs. Pray, "Lord, let them know the power of Your love for them."

- Forgive yourself. Our emotional state is not a punishment for our sins. This is really important! Too often people interpret what is going on in their lives by rationalizing, "I guess God is punishing me. So I have to be miserable or sad or depressed or unhappy in some way - or frightened. It's a punishment." It's not a punishment.

- We need to learn how to love as He loved and we can't do it without the Holy Spirit. We need to love unconditionally the way He loves us and He gives us the power to do that. Pray, "Lord, help me to love as You love"

- We need to repent. Let Him look into our hearts and reveal the sin that we need to repent so that we can surrender further.

- We need to be committed. I'm seeing a lack of commitment even among Christians. People aren't committed as much to their churches, their communities, their husbands, wives or children. People are becoming more selfish. Removing ourselves from the center and allowing Christ to be the focus of our lives brings peace and joy.

- We need to act. We're often better at lip service. Healing takes place only when we leave those safe little hiding places, away from grace, that we have built for ourselves. We have to come out into the Light, to throw off those tattered security blankets of fear, distrust, and unforgiveness. Healing will take place, even if we don't immediately recognize it.

- Read 2 Corinthians 8-9, " *You are well acquainted with the favor shown to you by our Lord Jesus Christ - how for your sake, he made himself poor though he was rich, so that you might become rich by his poverty.*"

- Before we leave this chapter on matters of the heart, I urge you to sit down and prayerfully write a long letter to God. Make a list of every time that you have had your heart broken. Regarding each of these incidents, try to remember and list what types of changes you made in your life afterwards to avoid another broken heart. It is only after recognizing and identifying our protective barriers that we can hope to tear them down. It can be a lengthy process, so try to be patient and include the Lord as you take it one step at a time. Consider discussing this letter with your spouse, confessor, or counselor.

Chapter 6

Body Enslavement

Rom 6:16 – *"You realize that when you offer your-selves to someone as obedient slaves, you are the slaves of the one you obey"*. Know your condition!

Our consumer society daily brainwashes us to obey our bodies at all costs.

Imagine a grand conspiracy deviously designed to put cravings and needs into your body. Welcome to America, land of the free and the home of the greatest consumer society ever created by humankind. The strat-egy of marketing is to create desire in the minds of poten-tial consumers. Madison Avenue spends billions designed to make you feel like your body needs constant and im-mediate gratification.

Think how many times a day you are told that things go better with Coke, that you deserve a break to-day, and that your weekends go way better if you get blitzed with Michelob. The makers of Sprite are currently spending tens of millions of dollars to repetitively send us the message, "Obey your thirst."

They're getting pretty good at telling us to obey our bodies. More than one thousand advertising messages reach most of us EACH DAY. You might literally wake up to a commercial on the clock radio. There are advertising messages in your morning newspaper and even on the back of the cereal box. You might switch on the TV to get some news while you get dressed in the latest fashions that are being advertised on morning television. You drive to work in a car you can't afford and pass countless billboards and signs all telling you what you ought to crave.

You get the idea. A zillion times each day we are told that if it feels good, do it. Obey the body!

You are bombarded with one-sided messages. For example, when was the last time you turned on the TV or opened a newspaper that suggested that prayer and fasting might be more effective routes to happiness than Pepsi or Chalupas.

But God whispers to us in Romans… *"you are the slaves of the one you obey."*

We need to know our condition. We need to know who is enslaving us. What are they telling us to do? Most of the time we don't have a clue, we just blindly follow, like so many hypnotized zombies believing the subliminal messages that society sends us.

Who do we obey? Do we obey food, alcohol, drugs, fear, depression, anxiety, friends, lovers, marriages, unforgiveness, and on and on? We need to open our minds, hearts, and souls and truly examine what masters we serve. To what or to whom have we enslaved ourselves? That is what we need to ask God to uncover as we read this chapter.

Our culture teaches us that every whim of the body needs to be taken care of immediately. I watched a television news magazine show recently. It was about people who have chosen to be "born again virgins" The Hollywood reporters pretty obviously thought that anyone choosing abstinence from sex was crazy. They said, "I don't understand, why are you giving up having sex with people? How can you give it up?"

God's will for us is abundant life. Does anyone reading this truly believe in his or her heart that the key to abundant life is free sex? The truth is that God advises us against those relationships. We need to keep ourselves chaste. No one watching prime time network television would guess that, in reality, casual sex hurts our self-esteem and damages our hearts. The truth is that self-esteem is not something that we can go out and buy, or obtain by sleeping with someone. Joyful and abundant living is not something that you can buy or pursue. It comes only as a byproduct of doing the next right thing, of making the right choices.

But the world is so cock-eyed that it can't understand why anyone would choose to be celibate. Eat, drink, and be merry because the credit card bill won't come until tomorrow. Madison Avenue just can't grasp the benefit that comes from NOT obeying the body. Well, maybe they can grasp it, but there's simply too much money to be made in the business of creating expensive and unquenchable desires.

I was coming back from St. Petersburg, Florida. One of the men from the seminary was being ordained as a deacon and a friend and I were driving home. Less than an hour from home, she said, "There's a Wendy's. Maybe I'll just pull in." So with my stomach rumbling, I said, "Yeah, great! That's fine."

So we pulled into Wendy's, quickly got out, got our food, got back in the car, sped off, and started filling ourselves with fat and salt. Our bodies told us we were hungry. Our bodies told us that the road to happiness is via burgers and fries. We didn't even want to wait another hour to get home and really sit down and have a meal. Fast food, fast cars, fast women, immediate gratification. Hungry, boom, gotta have it, gotta have it now, and gotta have it my way.

Remember when we talked about holding things up to scripture to see if they are true? Try holding instant gratification up to scripture. The tale of Job comes to mind. Patience and perseverance as spiritual principles come to mind. Psalm 36 talks about being patient, ignoring the quick success of ungodly people, and waiting for the Lord.

We are not accustomed to waiting. We are slaves to instant gratification. If we have a headache, immediately we'll take a tablet. If we can't sleep, we have a capsule. We have a pill for everything. Now there is even a pill, I don't know if anyone has seen this, called "Exercise In A Bottle!" They're fooling us and we're buying it. They've successfully taught us to look for the quick fix. We can't stand to have our bodies uncomfortable for even a second.

Our bodies have become gods, we have learned to blindly serve their every want and need. We have been taught so well that we wouldn't even think to procrastinate. Our worship and gratification of the body god is immediate.

The body says, "Feed me, and hurry up."
We say, "Yes master."

78

We don't have to be deep thinking philosophers to already know that superficial stuff doesn't bring us happiness. Our body urges us to "Feed me. Pleasure me. Make me feel perfect."

Have you ever actually met or even read of anyone who achieved joy and peace by pleasuring his or her bodies? How come so many rock and roll stars tend to kill themselves? How come the divorce rate skyrockets among big lottery winners? Why did Mother Theresa obviously have spiritual abundance even though she took vows of poverty and chastity?

No matter how many "better living through chemistry" commercials we hear, we already know that drugs will not bring us abundant life even if they come in a pretty hand-painted bottle with vintage years. We also know deep down that the phenomenal sex life of a movie star or NBA player is hollow and empty.

The other day I spoke to a middle-aged woman whose mother had suffered a stroke and who had moved in with the daughter. Having a sickly parent as a permanent guest put great stress on her and her husband. Do you know how she chooses to deal with it? She escaped each day to a local supermarket where she would buy half a dozen donuts and would wash them down with a quart of milk in the parking lot.

In her mind, she rationalized that she would "reward" her body for becoming her mother's caregiver. Isn't it amazing how blind we are to the damage we do by trying to satisfy cravings? Maybe the idea that donuts bring happiness is the reason that Krispy Kreme stock is doing so well.

Similarly, none of us make the conscious decision to become an alcoholic or drug addict. Yet how many of us seek happiness there? "If it feels good, do it." Instead of providing the happiness and fullness we crave, drugs and alcohol often kill us. What feels good is not necessarily good for us.

Hold the lies up to scripture to tell whether they are truth or not. God never said that everything was going to feel good. Can you imagine Jesus teaching that pleasuring our bodies would bring us inner peace? Can you imagine respecting anyone selling that? So why do we buy it?

Jesus said that we would suffer! Paul tells us in Romans, *"The tendency of the flesh is toward death."*

And in John 6, we read, *"It is the Spirit that gives life; the flesh is useless."*

Every time we give in to our body, in an unhealthy way, we die a little bit more. That's not dying of self. We surrender to untruth a little bit more each time we act on the lie. So we have to learn ways not to give into gluttony, lust, addiction, or more subtle slaveries to our bodies.

We know that God wants us free. He wants us to live this life in freedom. He has already given us the key to unshackle ourselves from all types of slavery. We have the tools to dismantle the blocks we build against grace. Salvation is ours, but so many of us are still living a life in bondage. So many of us have become enslaved to our bodies, apparently believing the Madison Avenue line that sex and conspicuous consumption leads to happiness.

I love to tell this story about a bear. There was a large old bear in a zoo and he was living in a cage that was six feet by six feet by six feet. All he ever did was pace back in forth in his small cage. As zoos have become more enlightened in modern times, they said, "No, we can't have this. This bear has to be released in a nature preserve."

They brought the bear in the cage to the place where he was going to be released. The community that gathered said, "Wow! This is great. We're going to open the gate and this bear is going to be so thrilled to be out in the wilderness that he is just going to frolic and run and be joyful." But when they opened the gate, the bear continued to pace back and forth…. six feet, six feet, six feet, six feet.

The gate was open, so they decided that maybe if they put food outside, the bear would come out. So they put food outside and the bear paced six feet, six feet, six feet, six feet inside the cage. Finally, they had to actually pull the cage away from him so that he would be outside in the wilderness. Even when they forcibly took the cage away, and put him in the middle of an open field, they found that he walked six feet, six feet, six feet and six feet.

Humans do the same thing. Our cage has been opened by His death and resurrection. Jesus himself coaches us out, yet we still continue to do the same walk. He pulled the cage away and we still remain stuck in old behavior. We have to move outside of the cage and out

81

into the freedom that Christ wants us to have. Surrender allows us to do that - to walk out in freedom.

To get a glimpse of how caught up in our bodies we seem to be, it is helpful to look at other cultures. I have been fortunate to accompany medical missions that go to Central America. These people, like people in most third world countries, have relatively nothing of material value. But they have a passion and a freedom that is so attractive because they do not get caught up in their bodies.

It didn't matter what size clothing they wore. In this culture people are not so concerned about what they wear, with how their hair is combed, or with the size of their bodies. The journey of their day was to find enough food to feed the people in their homes at least a little bit. Most of the time they couldn't even do that. Despite their struggles, in some ways they are so much freer than we often are. They aren't imprisoned. They do what they need to and they know in their every fiber that God is with them. They just don't get caught up in the same trivial things that enslave so many of us.

One Guatemalan friend on the trip has lived in the United States for a year or two where it is easy to become accustomed to material wealth. . We visited his mother in Central America and he said, "Mom, coming back here, now I realize that you are really under a lot of stress." And she said, "What is that? What is stress?" That was just life to her. You do the things you have to do. The average poor Guatemalan is probably less stressed out than their neurotic counterparts in Manhattan.

When I was in the countryside, the home where I stayed looked up the side of a mountain. Every morning

82

at about six, I would see a group of young children coming down a path. Later, I learned that they lived in a hamlet about a mile up the slope. The children come down the mountain to catch a bus to school. They didn't get back home again until it was dark, and then they would walk back up the mountain. But it wasn't a trial for them. They played and pushed each other and had fun while they walked. I loved watching them because life wasn't a problem for them and they were so happy. They weren't caught up in this body of theirs. We're so caught up in materialism that it's imprisoning us.

So we need to look at, "Who is our master?

Philippians 4:6 clearly states – *"Dismiss all anxiety from your minds. Present your needs to God in every form of prayer and in petition full of gratitude. Then God's own peace which is beyond all understanding, will stand guard over your hearts and minds in Christ Jesus."*

I remember a woman I worked with who was so anxious, so caught up in anxiety, because she had a shame that she was holding onto from her youth. She was a survivor of incest and she really believed that if someone found out about what had happened to her, then they wouldn't like her anymore. "What will people think if they know? What will they think?" She was so caught up in it...that anxiety ruled her life.

We need to walk out of that prison, out of that cage that we've been living in. We can be totally free.

I recently had the absolute blessing of giving a day of reflection to a group called Handicapped for Christ. There were about 125 of the most incredibly beautiful and joy-filled people. Joy-filled! I gave one of my talks and

83

as I was walking back to my table, this young man was calling out my name, "Carol, Carol!" I didn't hear him at first, because I don't hear well. So finally I turned and there was a paraplegic and he was lying on a bed. So I went over to him and he said, "Just come right down here; I just want to give you a hug because I know you need a hug." I said, "Oh, thank you!" I thought, "Look at this. He knew I needed a hug." I would have looked at him and thought that he needed a hug. But he didn't. I needed a hug. It was so beautiful.

A man who struggles with cerebral palsy then got up to witness. He was able to walk with a cane, but he didn't have great muscle or speech control. He shared how, three years prior to this particular date, he accepted Jesus into his life. He now calls himself a "free man." He said, "I am so free because Jesus is a part of my life." That is true freedom. We forget that when we get caught up in the body; we become slaves to the needs of our body. We really have to look at those areas that continue to enslave us.

Romans 7:24-25 – *"Who can free me from this body under the power of death? All praise to God through Jesus Christ our Lord."*

Even though his body didn't look free, this man was so free.

When I was there, the Lord put something on my heart. It was one of those days that I was wild. Once the Spirit hits, I can't stay still. I kept hearing the word "able body." "We need an *able body* over here," or "We need an *able body* at this table." The able bodies were those people that would volunteer their time to push wheel chairs and do different things during the day. When I

84

heard that, something in my spirit was upset and God put on my heart, "Everybody is an able body in Christ." We're all able-bodies. Because if He called us to serve in the womb (Isaiah 49:5), then we're all able bodies.

So when I got up to speak, I said, "There are no handicapped in Christ. We are all able bodies - every one of us. We each have a mission that we need to fulfill - every single one of us." The joyful cheering that came out of these people was unreal. I think they were tired of hearing it too - able bodies and handicapped. We are all able bodies. It doesn't matter what we look like. It doesn't matter how we move. It doesn't matter what we say. In reality, God put us here for whatever reason. We have to look at that for ourselves and we have to look at that with people that we minister to, because very often they are the ones that are actually ministering to us. When we start to look at people and say, "Aw, poor thing?"... That is the one that is going to be ministering to us.

We need to praise Him through the hurt and the depression and the desire to overeat or to drink or to control others. We need to praise Him through all of that and say, "You know, Lord, I'm not going to make any of these my master anymore. You are my Master." Some people, if they fall off the wagon, whatever that wagon might be, they beat themselves up. Our attitude needs to be that it's as important to learn and grow from one's mistakes as it is from our successes.

We have to be very careful not to stay focused on the sins of men, or the bad choices that we make, or the ugliness in our life. We have to force ourselves to stay focused on the glory of God. We've learned how to stay focused on the problems, but that doesn't get us past the problems. Staying focused on the glory of God gets us past the problems, because He is the one who knows how to get us past them. We don't know how to do that by ourselves and that's why we need to stay connected with Him. The alternative is to keep doing the same old things on self will, with the same old negative results.

I think of Shadrach, Meshach, and Abednego in the book of Daniel, and how they were thrown into the caldron. They didn't say, "Oh, I'm burning. I'm so hot. I'm burning my feet. Oh, somebody help me. Get me out of here." No, they said, "Praise the Lord! Praise the Lord!" And the Lord was there with them. The walls of Jericho – they came tumbling down. What walls do we have in our lives that need to come tumbling down? Whatever they are, or whatever fire we're thrown into... the truth is, the reality is, God's there. We just have to see Him. We never have to go through anything alone.

Look for the Lie
I often ask my patients to look for the lie. When did the lie start in your life? We pray and we look at that moment of pain in their life and we look for Jesus in the environment. I say, "Find Jesus in that environment. Where is He?" The patient finds that Jesus is there. We have to find Him and then stay focused on Him, because He's going to say, "Come on, come this way, come this way. Don't step there. Come. Come on. Come this way."

But instead, we stay focused on, "I'm here. I'm stuck. I did it again. Poor me." We beat ourselves up and we stay stuck. And that little troll on the side of the road is saying, "I did it again. I stopped them from coming over the bridge." We need to run past him. Just like Shadrach, Meshach, and Abednego, we want to overcome. We don't want to look for the quick fix anymore. We don't need to do that, because we have a God who doesn't want

86

to quick fix. He wants to "wholly fix." He wants to make us whole and to help us stay that way. That's what He wants for us.

Becoming Master of Your Body Exercises

- For one day, try keeping a "Body Log." Every time your body issues you a command, write it down. You might be surprised how much like a two year old it sounds with a constant, "I want this. I want chocolate. It's too hot in here. It's too cold. I am sleepy. I want coffee. I don't feel well. I want a pill. I want sex. I am tired and want to go home. I am bored. I want a cigarette. I want a glass of wine. I want more comfortable clothes and softer furniture. I want. I want. I want. Look for trends. Try to identify the difference between cravings/desires and needs. Every time you surrender to a craving of your body, the cravings grow stronger! Every time you say "no", your spirit grows stronger.

- Try meditation. Read a few passages from the bible or inspiration book and sit for twenty minutes trying not to think about a thing. Make yourself a vessel of the Lord. Don't give into the body by squirming or scratching for the full 20 minutes. If you can't make the full twenty minutes, instead of beating yourself up, try five minutes and then progress from there.

- If you have problems with drugs, alcohol, or over-eating….look in the white pages of your local phone book and check out Alcoholics Anonymous, Narcotics Anonymous, or Overeaters

Anonymous. Try open-mindedly attending a meeting everyday for a week. All of these programs are God-based spiritual programs. The twelve steps of recovery are bible-based ways to heal through God's grace.

 Chapter 7

Malnourished Souls

If you want to know the condition of your soul, then go look in the mirror and ask yourself whether you are looking at:

    a) A spiritually nourished person.

or

    b) A person in need of spiritual nourishment.

Grace is the only thing that nourishes the soul. No matter what else we try to feed it, the only thing that our souls can digest is God's good grace. Forget about chitlins and black eye peas....grace is the ultimate and only soul food.

Our souls crave. Our souls yearn. It's amazing what we try in silly attempts to nourish the soul.

For example, I read an article in a magazine recently about a very financially successful woman who has risen to the position of President and CEO of one of the world's foremost publishing companies. In the interview, despite being a wife and mother to a 15-year-old daughter, she admitted working an insane amount of hours – more than one hundred per week. Listen to this quote, it floored me, "My family is supportive of my workaholism", she said. **"They know this is how I get my <u>soul satisfaction</u>."**

It's amazing how far we get from truth when we try to fill our souls with work, money, sex, drugs, rock and roll. I am not trying to pick on a single executive, to some extent we all do this. How many of us unconsciously think, "If only I had a newer car then I would feel better inside." Maybe you are like so many and there is a little voice inside that says, "Maybe if I have that second piece of chocolate, then I will feel better inside."

While our executive tries to fill her empty soul with work, what do you think the chances are that she is actually satisfying her soul? As her life flashes before her eyes on her deathbed, do you suppose she will regret not spending more time at the office? Regret dying without more money in the bank? Or do you suppose she will think about her daughter growing up in her difficult teen years without a mom.

The cover design of this book is meant to depict a human soul at least partially blocked off from grace. Remember, it's grace and only grace that nourishes our souls. The irony in the CEO example is that in the process of trying to satisfy her soul, she ends up starving it by blocking herself off from her daughter and those who love her. She blocks herself from that which she needs most – soul nourishment. This is something we all do at times.

The soul gets nourishment from God and in return it nourishes us. It's our very life spirit. Imagine that part of ourselves, that inner spiritual core, that gets touched by an act of love or refreshed from prayer and meditation. The part of us that responds to beauty and goodness. When the soul is healthy, it invigorates us, it give us life, it makes us glow, it gives us zeal and contentment that is not phased by the day to day minutia of material life.

Inappropriately responding to that yearning inside by trying to feed it a porn movie, an hour of Jerry Springer, juicy gossip, a six pack of beer, or a bar of Godiva chocolate just isn't going to do it.

An unhealthy soul is a Catch 22. If you build protective umbrellas or shields between yourself and God, the result is an unhealthy soul. This hurts us. As we have previously discussed, when we are hurt we tend to back away even farther from God and from others. The cycle can only be broken by God's grace.

Not enough truth has been written about the soul and the stuff that is written often misleads us.

I looked for another quote about soul in this week's news and found a beauty from Cristina Aguilera. After appearing with other girl rockers in a particularly titillating video, called "Get Your Ya Ya's Out", dripping with sex, she said, "I hope you like it. We put our souls into it."

I am not sure if the divas put their souls into it, but it's certain they put an awful lot of their bodies into it.

So it's no surprise that we rarely think about the true nature or the health of our souls. The purpose of this short chapter is simple, to get you to ask the question: "What is the condition of my soul?"

Early in my practice I started seeing patterns of low-lying depression, unresponsiveness to others, and a general lack of zeal for the Lord's work even among good Christians. There was no apparent psychological or physiological reason for this spiritual malaise.

I started to research and that's when I came across a few different books including a very interesting work by Douglas Rumford called Soul Shaping.

Let me quote here from Mr. Rumford, "Eternity is a quality of life that begins now. Eternity in our hearts means that we intuitively know that we were made for a life of meaningful relationships, for higher purposes beyond our own success, and for a sense of connection with the Creator and Designer of the universe."

So the work of the soul is knowing that there is much more to life than what we can see. Knowing that God is good all of the time, no matter what I'm going through, is the role of the soul. The soul is central to the spiritual virtue of acceptance.

Rumford also states, "The life that most satisfies is rooted firmly in the soul and is nurtured by faith."

When we are fully satisfied, we know that our soul is healthy. That doesn't mean that everything has to be going swimmingly in our lives, because that's rare (if all is wonderful in your life, don't worry, this too shall pass). Christian serenity doesn't mean having faith and loving the Lord only when everything is going well. It means being fully satisfied in our day-to-day lives full of kids crying, bosses bossing, and spouses spouting off.

Like the poor always among us, there will always be something there to challenge us. There are always things that are thrown at us, but we see beyond that. When my children call with a problem or with a situation that they are dealing with in school or at work, I say, "Put on the eyes of a prophet, and look beyond the flesh. Look beyond what you see happening in this particular situation. Now what does God show you?" And every time – every time – they'll come back and say, "Wow, you know Mom, God showed me that this is really what the situation is, and it doesn't bother me anymore that this is happening at work or at school." We need to put on the eyes of a prophet and look beyond our circumstances. A healthy soul allows us to do that.

When our soul is damaged and needs healing, it hungers and yearns. Unfortunately, very often we feed it with the wrong stuff. Sometimes we listen to the voice of our body…instead of listening to the infinitely wise voice of The Lord as He whispers to our soul.

Rumford calls it "spiritual hypothermia." If someone is out in the cold, when hypothermia sets in, they'll say to themselves, "Oh, if only I could just rest for a little while, then I know I'll have the strength to go on." They get tired, they fall asleep in the snow bank, and they freeze to death. That rest kills! Sometimes our instincts are just plain wrong. Mild depression urges us to stay in bed, the very opposite of taking therapeutic action.

It's the same thing that happens with the soul. I have patients, good Christian patients, who come in all the time and say things like, "I was unhappy in my marriage and I recognize that I was pulling away from my wife because I wasn't feeling satisfied in the marriage. So I had an affair and I feel good now that I had this affair."

93

You thought it might be nice, but just like laying down in a snow bank, it invites death. You thought the affair would be fulfilling, but that's only an illusion. "Ah, if only I had sex with that person...then I would feel all right inside." You know, Satan will give us our desires. He'll do whatever it takes to try and draw us into sin. Misery loves company. In contrast, God wants us to have and abundant and joyous life.

OK, so you don't cheat on your spouse but you can experience the same things with material wants. "If only I had that new car, then I would be happy inside." That "new car" happiness only lasts about a week or two. It's an illusion of soul satisfaction. New cars, more sex, more power, prestige....we are trying to satisfy something deep within our souls, and a shopping spree at the mall or watching a soap opera on the tube just isn't going to do it.

To live fully alive in Christ Jesus is to give up on the illusions of self- protection or self-fulfillment and to give into God's love for me. To accomplish this, I have to look at the soul, that quiet voice that is inside of me. If I'm afraid to do that, worried about "Oh, what am I going to find out?"... then most of the time we're going to find a soul that is damaged. There needs to be a healing.

Zeal
The one word that describes the soul best, something that we can latch onto and understand, is the word, "ZEAL." A healthy soul manifests itself in our zeal for the Lord, for life, and for human relationships.

We need to recognize as Christians that when our salvation is not overflowing into how we live, how we minister to others, and how we view the world around us, then something is wrong. A healthy soul has a zeal for God's work and a compassion that exceeds all understanding of compassion. Mother Theresa, with her love and compassion, knew without doubt that there was a bigger picture to life. As a result, she was the epitome of tireless zeal.

The soul can only be healed by God. You can't walk into a therapist's office or even into spiritual direction to have your soul fixed. You have to sit at the foot of God and allow Him to come into those areas of your life that need to be healed. That is why it is so important to identify and dismantle the blocks outlined in this book.

Very often I'll tell parents to write letters to their kids, even adult kids, same as I do with couples, asking their forgiveness for things that they did. Their souls are healed through that.

I had one patient that I'll never forget – I asked him to write this letter to his son, and he said, "You know, my son and I have a wonderful relationship." I said, "I know that because I've seen you together." His son was about thirty-five years old. "But the Lord is just putting it on my heart that there is something more." So he said okay. He prayed, wrote a letter, and gave it to his son.

His son said, "But Dad, you don't have to apologize for anything. I know I was a rough teenager." His dad said, "No, I want you to read this letter." And he did. At our next session the father told me, "I don't know what happened, because my son was affectionate to me and loving, but ever since that letter, our relationship is different. There is something that has changed. God healed us." He didn't even know it was broken. That, to me, is the healing of the soul. It goes beyond what we know, beyond what we can see or touch, into an area that we're not familiar with... the realm of the soul.

The soul is that river, a river that always needs to be filled. If we consciously or unconsciously damn that river with our blocks, and it dries up, then we don't have that same excitement for the Lord. We don't have that same zeal for either life or the Lord.

In John 7:37 we read, *"If any man is thirsty, let him come to me and drink. He who believes in me, as the Scripture said, from his innermost being shall flow rivers of living water."*

"Shall flow rivers?" This means that life-giving water has to be flooding. We have to look and ask, "Is my tank empty, or is it full? Do I have Living Water flowing through me?" It's raining down grace all around, while so many of us hide under umbrellas.

Just like spiritual hypothermia, we binge. This is from Rumford again – "We binge on sin when we are starved for grace." How true! We start giving into the body, one vice leads to another, and sin so often dominoes. We turn away from God rather than turning toward Him when we are hungry or hurting in some way. It's the soul that craves, that yearns to be filled with grace, that cries and aches to be healed.

So we need to know, "What is the condition of my soul?" We can't intellectualize the soul. We can, however, recognize that we were created to be one body in Christ with gifts and talents that are desperately needed in the community. If the river runs dry, our will to continue to love is diminished. We need to strive for "self-less" love rather than self-absorbed love.

In the Trust chapter we discussed how people sometimes have knowledge of God on some level, but just don't have the deep experience of that knowledge. So many haven't yet embraced the fullness of that experience.

If our souls are unhealthy or in need of lifting up (as the Scriptures say) then everything we think and feel can be distorted by painful memories that have drained the soul of its life-giving flow. Our will and our behavior then are outward expressions of that distortion. That's why we intelligent people tend to do dumb things like trying to fill our souls with workaholism, alcoholism, shopping or jelly donuts.

I often think about how blessed I was to be raised in a loving nurturing home. As I grow older, I realize more and more how much of a blessing this still is. My parents were not religious nor did they go to church. However, when I look back on my childhood, the love that they shared and the love they showed me was very Christ-like. They nurtured, they empowered, they played, they laughed, they disciplined, they embraced, they answered questions and they asked questions. Always with respect and love for who I was.

I know now that my soul's understanding of those memories allowed me to desire and strive for God's will in my life. What they did and how they raised me was of God's design. They, in essence, gave me the ability to hunger and thirst for God. My soul was being fed with that which is right and just in God's eyes. I knew I was God's Beloved--- because as a child I was their beloved--- I didn't have the baggage many have. My river was constantly being filled. They never knew what the impact of their love would have on me, an impact that I am hopefully still daily passing on to my family, friends, students, and patients.

When you are looking in the mirror and examining your soul, here are some things to look for:

- Look at low levels of depression, when the joy of the Lord is not filling you. I don't mean a situational depression or clinical depression. I mean when you're going through life, and things are basically okay, but you're not experiencing the joy of the Lord. That is usually one sign of a soul that needs to be healed.

- Boredom – With a healthy soul, we're never bored with God's work. Never, never, never bored! There's no time to be bored. When you are experiencing boredom, that usually is an indication that your soul needs to be healed, because otherwise, you would have that energy, you'd have that zeal to do whatever it is that God calls you to do. Because we have a job – every one of us.

- Inactivity or overly busy with just busyness. Some soul-sick people just sit and don't want to do anything. Others choose to escape in busyness. Remember our workaholic executive who ignores her family and actually thinks she is feeding her soul? The best way to nurture our soul is to sit quietly before the Lord and ask Him for nourishment, healing, and the zeal to carry out His will for us.

- If old unhealthy behaviors suddenly surface, consider that you might be inappropriately trying to fill a soul that needs filling with grace instead.

- If we start feeling a lack of self-control and start to give in to sinful behavior, it may be a sign that our soul needs attention. We need to place ourselves before Him for healing.

- Withdrawal from responsibility One woman I remember, a leader in the charismatic renewal, said, "I don't care anymore. If someone comes to me and is broken – something that I would have sat and cried about with them in the past – I don't care anymore. It disturbs me that I don't have some feeling of wanting to nurture them. I just don't care anymore." She and her soul needed to be healed. Restlessness and dissatisfaction, feelings that nothing is right, can tell us that our souls need filling. If we find ourselves thinking or commenting things like, "What a horrible sermon, can't he get it right?" or "Look at this prayer group; it's just dwindling to nothing. I'm just so aggravated," We need to pay attention to our soul.

So we need to allow the Holy Spirit to penetrate those areas of our mind, our body, our heart, and our soul. We need to expose the areas where healing is needed. Remember this is a process...not instant bells and whistles gratification. If you have read this far, I know He is already doing it for you. He will continue His work in you. But don't ignore your soul.

99

Every single day, pray for your soul. You're speaking to your soul. You're calling upon God's grace to restore your soul. You need to pray specifically that God restores, nourishes, and fills your soul.

[Psalm 108:3] *Awake, my soul; awake, lyre and harp! I will wake the dawn.*

[Psalm 16:9] *Therefore my heart is glad, my soul rejoices; my body also dwells secure,*

[Psalm 25:1] *I wait for you, O LORD; I lift up my soul*

[Psalm 34:3] *My soul will glory in the LORD that the poor may hear and be glad.*

Psalm 42 - *My soul thirsts for you, O God*

[Jer 31:25] *For I will refresh the weary soul; every soul that languishes I will replenish.*

[Luke 1:46] And Mary said: "*My soul proclaims the greatness of the Lord;*

[Is 26:9] *My soul yearns for you in the night,*

Allow yourself, as difficult as it may be at first, to sit quietly before the Lord. Find yourself a special place where it's just you and God. Whether it's a beach or a prayer chapel or a meditation garden or your bedroom doesn't matter so much as your willingness. Don't be afraid of the silence. Savor it. Silence is so rare in our society, and even in our church services. Picture David sitting in watch of his sheep. Clear your mind; the only sound is that of the breath of God in the air that surrounds him. How glorious are your works oh Lord, how precious your gifts.

Lord there is a wonderful gift in your silence. It is in that silence that we hear Your voice in the depth of our soul. It is in that silence that we can hear You call our

100

name, call us your beloved. Lord, I pray that all who call upon you today experience a restoration of their soul. Bring each soul back to wholeness. Father God, in the name of Your son Jesus and through the power of the Holy Spirit I pray living water to flow freely and completely. Amen.

Chapter 8

Family Tree

Another area that blocks us from fully walking in the fullness of Christ is our ancestry. This is probably the last place most people would look for a blockage from grace.

You, each and every one of you, can be a channel of grace in healing present and future generations. The object of this chapter is to get you to at least think about your "trans-generational" connection. The ripples that reach out from our each and every action run much deeper and farther than most of us imagine. For example, something extraordinarily kind or loving that you do for your child today can conceivably make an impact that will touch your grandchildren.

In my practice, I have noticed that things like divorce, sexual abuse, addiction and other calamities seem to run in families just like red hair or freckles. Something a bit deeper than just genetics alone or family tradition alone is at work.

People will say to themselves, "Oh I accepted the Lord in my life thirty or forty years ago, so none of that old baggage is going to bother me anymore." Well, whether we modern sophisticates understand it or not, Scripture tells us that the sins of our fathers are passed down. It isn't the sin itself that is passed down, but rather the ramifications of that sin.

If you read Nehemiah 9, it goes through a whole litany of how God forgives the people and then they stiffen their necks again and tighten up their backs and do the same rebellious act over and over. God forgives them but they do it again, and then He forgives them but they do it again.

I think some of us are still experiencing the fallout from those kinds of sins. The truth is that God only wants the best for us, but when we continue to choose sin and become slave to that sin, then we're not having abundant life.

Perhaps a scientist might say that we have genetic predispositions to sin...some of us more than others. The bottom line is that this is a useful area to explore in our quest for grace.

2 Peter 2:19 – *"For surely anyone is slave of that by which he has been overcome."*

We're a society, a culture that cultivates sinfulness. Prime time television doesn't exactly cultivate holiness. That's why, very often, we don't even recognize what's happening, because we are so accustomed to it. We've learned from our first parents, Adam and Eve, to be self-absorbed. And I don't mean this in a personal way; I mean collectively. We've been taught that we have to take care of number one.

In reality, though, the world's view is not truth. The truth is that God's word tells us that we are our brother's keeper. So we can't just take care of number one and expect to achieve fulfillment.

Sometimes we need to be responsible to one another on a physical level. We need to help people – to feed them – to take care of their physical or personal needs. We are also all connected on a spiritual level.

We call this interdependence. We become interdependent on one another. Now, instead, what we hear all the time, especially women, "You need to be independent – be an independent thinker and an independent woman." What the heck does that mean? Are we supposed to leave everybody behind? No, God says we need to be interdependent on one another. We are in this together.

Pope John XXIII made the statement, "We are all saved and sanctified in clusters like grapes. No one goes to either heaven or hell alone. We are all in this together."

I think of the ramifications of sin when I see a family where sexual sin is rampant. If you are not a counselor or confessor, then you might not have any idea of just how pervasive incest and adultery have become in our society.

The damage caused by sexual sin is incredible. Many times my patients rationalize that they are the only ones being hurt. Obviously, though, it takes more than one person to commit adultery. Of course, each person in an adulterous relationship also has a family and a circle of friends that are impacted.

When a man or a woman chooses to commit adultery, his or her spouse is dragged to ground zero of the fallout. There's usually lots of anger and hurt. Very often, there is unforgiveness. The children, if any, are exposed to the mayhem. They learn ugly ideas about what relationships are all about. Children of divorced or adulterous parents are astronomically more likely to opt for divorce or adultery themselves.

So sin begets sin begets sin begets sin. It continues on and on. Although the family can be such a wonderful vehicle for grace, it can also be a vehicle for sin. So we have to look at that. "Is my family nurturing grace – is it a grace-filled environment - or is it continuing to nurture sin?"

Grace seems to run more in some families than in others. I think it's something we need to ask God to activate. God is steadily pouring an abundance of grace down upon us, all the time, but so many of us miss it while hiding under our umbrellas of anger, distrust, and unforgiveness. <u>A good spouse will help bring more grace to his or her partner than anything else.</u> That connectedness with one another is what marriage is all about.

We Are All Influenced By Our Family Tree

I worked with one woman who was raised in a satanic cult. Her dad was a Pentecostal minister during the day, and at night, he was a satanic priest. Now, needless to say, this young woman had a tremendous number of problems on a psychological level. On a spiritual level, she was in extreme bondage.

She came to church with us once and when she saw the altar setup with candles and a chalice, she panicked. She had to run out of there. She had so many skeletons to battle, so many things in her closet that she had to deal with. Every time her parents would send her a letter or call her on the phone, they would say, "I love you." That word "love" would put her in a panic. I knew when they said it on the phone because I would see her go blank. She would go stiff.

"Love" is such a beautiful word. But for her, it was an entrapment and she would just go terrifyingly rigid. She would absolutely freeze. I don't know what would come after that, what that word meant to her and where it would lead her, but she would always freeze. There were times when after hanging up the phone she would start to shake with fear, other times she would become very paranoid and still other times she would flash back into an earlier time in her life. The sad thing is that some of that baggage probably got passed down to her children...and perhaps even to her children's children and to their children and so on.

Then I think about my own sons. One of the things we always did before they left for school was that we prayed. Each one of us would take a turn asking Jesus to fill us with more of his Spirit. We would say, "Jesus, fill me with more of your Spirit. Jesus, fill me with more of your Spirit. Jesus, fill me with more of your Spirit." We would close the prayer with hugs and then they would leave.

Years later they told me about finding all sorts of alcohol, drugs, and sexual opportunities during college. They said, "You know, we knew that the two of you were praying for us, because we could always go just so far, and we couldn't step over that line. It was just so far." But they had prayed each day, "Lord, fill me with your Spirit." So, God did that. We were able to pass on the grace to them and they were able to continue to live in it when they were away at school.

There are two factors that influence us that we hear about all the time: heredity (our genetic nature) and environment (the way we were nurtured).

It is useful to know how our family tree affects us. We can get a clue by looking at Exodus 20 where God delivers the Ten Commandments. *"For I the Lord your God am a jealous God, inflicting punishment for their fathers' wickedness on the children of those who hate me, down to the third and fourth generation, but bestowing mercy down to the thousandth generation on the children of those who love me and keep my commandments."*

Wow! Generational bondage! So we are going to experience the effects of the sins or the faithfulness of parents and grandparents and great-grandparents and on and on and on. Think of it. Your decision and actions today, whether they involve adultery or volunteering in a soup kitchen, may pass down as either blessings or curses to your children and grandchildren to the third and fourth generations.

Numbers 14:18 – *"Even as you have said the Lord is slow to anger and rich in kindness, forgiving wickedness and crime, yet not declaring the guilty guileless, but punishing children to the third and fourth generation by their fathers' wickedness."*

Jeremiah 32:18 – *"You continue your kindness through a thousand generations and you repay their father's guilt, even into the lap of their sons who follow them."*

When I was born I was named Carol, which didn't fit with the names given to other family members. Others were named after somebody and I wasn't named after anyone. I didn't understand that. My mom said, "I named you Carol because I loved Christmas carols. They brought me such joy." That was a blessing. When she said that, she prayed a blessing over me. She didn't even know she was praying. Perhaps as a result of her blessing, I have always been able to approach difficulties with God's joy. Now I don't mean, "Yeah, oh please send on the trial." I mean knowing in the deepest part of my being that Jesus is always there through the process. So she spoke a blessing.

We Can Speak A Blessing Or We Can Speak A Curse

It's so sad to hear parents curse their kids. "You'll make nothing of yourself." And they make nothing of themselves. "You're a loser. You are stupid. You are ugly." We curse. We can curse or we can bless. We need to look at that, because again, it passes on and on and on. Once I heard a woman at the zoo say to her four-year-old, "Shut up or I will cut off your tongue and feed it to the animals." What are the ramifications of our words?

Lamentations 5:7 - *"Our fathers sinned and are no more and we bear their punishment."* The Scripture is clear – very clear.

There is an awful lot to family tree and I just want to cover it lightly here. I ask you to continue to reflect, think about family, ancestral healing, severing from the past, breaking the chain of the sins of the fathers that have been passed down, and for those things that I may inflict on future generations. Jesus is still the answer. He certainly reveals these things to us and he tells us, *"I am still the answer. I'm not leaving you out there alone."*

Ephesians 2:19-22 - *"You are fellow citizens of the saints and members of the household of God. You form a building which rises on the foundation of the apostles and prophets with Christ Jesus himself as the capstone. Through him, the whole structure is fitted together and takes shape as a holy temple in the Lord. In him, you are being built into this temple to become a dwelling place for God in the Spirit."*

To truly celebrate this time in the Lord, and to walk in His fullness, we need to look at these areas in our lives that are keeping us stuck. If it is our family tree, if it is our soul that needs healing, if it is our body that keeps getting us in trouble, our heart that needs to be healed, our mind that is telling us things that just aren't true, and if we are not trusting or if we're not forgiving people in our life.... we need to look at these things and offer it to Him, because through that healing, we will be free to walk in His fullness!

Chapter 9

Toxic Unforgiveness

John 3:16 *"For God so loved the world that He gave His only son that whoever believes in him may not die but may have eternal life. God did not send the Son into the world to condemn the world, but that the world might be saved through him."*

Before we get into forgiveness, I think it is important for us to look at the paradox of "forgiving love." You can't have one without the other. You can't really separate them, although we are certainly going to get into the forgiveness part of it. But I'd like to look a little bit at the paradox, because God's concept of love and forgiveness is radically different from ours, and we really need to have an understanding of that difference.

Our concept of love is that we tend to love what we like. If we like something, then it's a lot easier to choose to love it. God's concept is that He loves what is in our best interest. There's a big difference.

Our concept is we're inclined to forgive only when it is in our best interest. But He wants us to forgive when it is in the best interest of someone else. Our concept is that we embrace what is comfortable and try to avoid pain. He tells us in Romans 12:9 – *"Let love be without hypocrisy; abhor what is evil. Cling to what is good.*" He didn't say that would happen without pain.

So loving requires us to forgive and forgiving requires us to love. It's not easy. It's a tough message but God commands us to forgive and to love. If we want the peace and joy of being God's children, then love and forgiveness are a crucial part of the price of admission. One cannot simultaneously call oneself a loving Christian while harboring unforgiveness. Unforgiveness is central to being a Christian.

The world knows we are Christians by our love, by our unconditional love. Sometimes we don't look any different than the rest of the world in the way we love, in the way we forgive. I know that many of you are not pleased with my strong words regarding harboring unforgiveness, but unforgiveness makes people so miserable and I see its cancerous tentacles keeping so many of my patients away from peace and serenity. The hard truth is that God commands us to forgive.

The good news is that when God commands us to do something, He gives us the tools to carry out His orders. He sends the Holy Spirit to strengthen us and whisper encouragement into our hearts. He gives us His loving grace to fill our souls up the brim. He gives us the grace to forgive others and He gives us His grace to forgive ourselves.

If you are one of those people who tends to beat yourself up, then you are not alone. Self-destructive behaviors of all types run rampant in our society and we can do a lot of damage to others and to ourselves. It's normally a whole lot easier to forgive someone else than it is to forgive yourself. Pray over this. This book is about tearing down the walls that block you from God and wiping clean your slate as God's child. God teaches us by example. God forgives your every sin. Unforgiveness is toxic and it is the opposite of love. As you walk with the Lord, and ask for healing and the grace to forgive yourself of anything that you might consciously or unconsciously still hold against yourself.

I looked in the dictionary for a definition of "give", because we hear that He gave His only Son. I wanted to get a better understanding of "give."

The dictionary says that "Give" means to: "make a present of, to yield to another, to put into the possession or keeping of another," and listen to this one - "to deliver in exchange."

God delivered His son in exchange for our sins. He delivered His son, and it was not a gentle handover. He didn't deliver Him like He would a present. He didn't deliver Him very nicely packaged wrapped up with a ribbon and bow. Instead it was very bloody. It was painful. It was a struggle, but He delivered Jesus in exchange for our sins.

The cross then brought us redemption. We have forgiveness through the cross. As Christians, because we have already received this forgiveness, we are obligated to extend it to others and to ourselves.

Isaiah 53:4 – *"Yet ours were the sufferings he was bearing, ours the sorrows he was carrying, while we thought of him as someone being punished and struck with affliction by God. Whereas, he was being wounded for our rebellions, crushed because of our guilt, the pun-*

113

ishment reconciling us fell on him, and we have been healed by his bruises."

We have been - that's past tense. We have been healed by his bruises! That scripture is overwhelming to me! It says so much. When I first came into the Spirit and started to recognize this God who loved me so much, I didn't understand Calvary. I don't know that we'll ever really understand it, but I prayed to the Lord, "I have to understand it more. I know You tell me that You did this for my sins, but I'm not a murderer. I never did anything so bad. So, was it really for me that You died? What are you forgiving in me?" I want to understand it. I was desperate to understand the cross.

Well, I didn't really understand what I was praying for at that particular time. I thought it was just kind of a general understanding prayer. I thought that He was just going to point out a text, and I'd have a better understanding of it. But it wasn't like that at all.

In fact, I was alone at home the day I prayed for knowledge of my sins and I was just sitting out in the patio. What He revealed to me brought me back to 1972 when Roe vs. Wade was first overturned. At that time we used to have these panel debates and I was on the pro-life panel. We would debate our opponents; at that time we called them pro-abortionists. I went to church in those days but I was certainly not in the Spirit. But I did believe that I was doing something for God.

However, at that time I had that real New York attitude. Not everything that came out of my mouth was very holy, unfortunately, and it wasn't presented in the kindest way. So, God brought me back to that point, and He showed me and revealed in my heart how many women I really had murdered with my words – you know, pointing at them and calling them "You murderers!" It wasn't very pleasant, and He showed me that.

The wonderful thing about our God - and how we can always tell when God is revealing something to us or if we are simply beating ourselves up – is that there was no condemnation. He didn't condemn me. He revealed it to show me, "Hey, you prayed for this; you want to know what I have forgiven you for. This is what it is." He revealed it, and for the first time I was able to see it.

I sobbed. I cried my heart out because I had self-righteously hurt so many people. I said, "O, Lord, I am so sorry. I am so sorry I did this. I did put that nail in you. I did that and I'm so sorry." I was just sobbing and sobbing.

Just then the phone rang. Any good therapist knows you just don't pick up the phone when you are sobbing. You don't do that. You are supposed to be in control, right? But it was a knee-jerk reaction. The phone rang. I picked it up. "Sob, sob, sob – Hello - sob, sob, sob."

It was a friend on the phone. Her name was Thelma. She said, "What the heck is wrong with you?" So I said, "Oh, Thelma, you can't believe this!" and I told her the whole story. I said, "I am so sorry. I am so sorry. I wish I had those women in front of me right now so I could say, 'I'm sorry for hurting you. I'm sorry!"

Without missing a beat, she said, "We forgive you, all of us." She told me, "I was one of those women back in 1972 and I almost took my life. It was by the grace of God that the handful of pills that I took didn't

115

work quickly enough and someone found me and brought me to the hospital." She said, "But I was one of those women. I was so desperate that I didn't think there was any other way and I had an abortion. But God redeemed me. He saved me. And for all of those women we accept your apology. We know that you didn't know any better."

I said, "Wow! What a God we have!" He brings us to that point and gives us exactly what we need. I was hurting. I was turned inside out. He brought me to that point and then He rescued me. I asked and was shown my guilt and was given a way to relieve it.

So when we ask these questions of Him, He answers. I didn't even know that I wasn't free. I was just asking a question. I think this is the trap we get into. We don't recognize that we are human beings and there is always something blocking us from the fullness of The Light. For me, this experience was a huge awakening. It made me so sensitive to my own condition, recognizing that I don't know everything that is going on within me. He has to reveal it to me. It has to come from Him. So I've become really open to anything He has to teach me.

My Daddy knew the depth of my heart. He knew my pain, my repentance, and He unconditionally forgave me. The good news was that I received His forgiveness instead of beating myself up. I knew that the God of Creation stepped into that moment of time with me and answered my prayer.

We have to look at those times when God steps into the moment with us and we have to listen. We have to listen because He is doing it for a couple of reasons. One - to get us through the pain and that is what He did for me. Secondly, and probably more importantly, to empower us to get out there and do the job we are supposed to be doing. We get stuck in our old ways. But, like little Simon Birch, we each have a job to do.

I believe without a shadow of a doubt that our world would not be in the condition it is now in if we, as believing Christians, would get out and do what we were called to do. Remember the scripture that we have each been called from the womb. Whatever our mission, He has to reveal it to us. He is the only one with the answer. The Lord will reveal it to us so long as we ask and are open to the answer.

We have a Daddy who is incredibly in love with us and He wants us to be all we can be. Turning our lives and our will over to the care of God means freedom and peace that surpasses all understanding as well as the overwhelming joy of being at one with The Lord.

I saw a family once at LaGuardia Airport in New York. There was a little girl running and playing. She was about two years old and she had two older sisters. They were all playing well together. The interaction that I really enjoyed watching was this little girl, Annie, and her dad. She would just kiss him and snuggle with him on his lap, then run and play, and then go back to the lap for more kisses and cuddles. She was calling him something and I couldn't hear it. God is so gracious because He knows how nosy I am and I wanted to know what she was calling him. So He brought them right in front of me and the little girl got stuck in those airport chairs that go back to back. Right in front of me, her dad came over and he just extended his hand because he was afraid she would get hurt. He extended his hand and he said, "Annie, come to Abba."

Come to Abba. Come to Papa. Come to Daddy. Don't you love that? Compare this trusting child's love with our love for God. We call Him Our Father. How formal and cold is that? I never called my dad, "Father." I called him "Daddy." I think our Father in Heaven wants that same intimate relationship that Annie and Abba enjoy.

God calls us into a "shalom." Shalom means wholeness in God, a peace that is overwhelming. Shalom peace allows us to come into that intimacy that is so close that we can sense His breathing. That is what He wants for us. It was for this intimate relationship with God that we were created.

Choosing Forgiveness

We want to understand the forgiveness that He has for us and then take that same forgiveness and extend it to others and to ourselves.

Matthew 6:14 – *"Your Heavenly Father will forgive you if you forgive those who sin against you, but if you refuse to forgive them, He will not forgive you."*

Mark 11:25 –*"But when you are praying, first forgive anyone you are holding a grudge against, so that your Father in Heaven will forgive you your sins too."*

We really need to read these Scriptures and understand that we have a part in this. We need to meet Him. We need to take what He has given us and extend it to others.

It is important to understand that forgiveness is an act of will. It is not a feeling. It's a choice we make using

118

our free will. We make a choice to forgive, and we don't always feel good about it, at least not right away. "I choose to forgive. Lord, you do the rest. You give me the grace to experience the freedom from that forgiveness. I'm going to line my will up with Yours." He honors that and gives us the freedom that comes from becoming unshackled from our resentments.

There are certainly some experiences in life that we have to look at and struggle with sometimes. We have to look at situations where we have been hurt and say, "Lord, I choose to forgive; let me look at the anger and hurt that has come from this."

I am not talking about just mumbling a general blanket statement, "Let's forgive," and act like it never happened. No, sometimes we have to look at things with a forgiving spirit and recognize that "I was hurt through it, but Lord, what can I learn from this? What is the understanding I can have from this?" We need to look at the times we were hurt in our life, and surrender those times to the Lord. The good news is that these are the times we probably have grown the most.

I know when I look at the times when I was hurt, when I believed that somebody wronged me in some way, and if I approached them in God's way with a forgiving heart, they were the most profound growth experiences in my life. They formed me into who I am today, and hopefully into who I will be as I continue to grow. When hurtful things are done to us, we can hold onto them, thereby paralyzing ourselves...or we can ask God's strength to forgive and grow in freedom.

Remember, forgiveness is an act of the will. That doesn't mean that we are not going to experience anger when we are hurt. But as Christians, when that anger starts to sting and the hurt starts to well us inside, pray for happiness and holiness for the person who has harmed you.

When I first heard this suggestion I said, "I don't want to do that. I don't want them to be happier and holier." Then I realized what was going on with me. I can choose to forgive and pray for good things for others, or I can choose to withhold forgiveness, to secretly wish hardship for others, and to be bitter and resentful. I have a choice – we all do. God's will for me is forgiveness because He wants me to be joyous and free...not bitter and unforgiving

Prayer is the answer to resentment. If we find that we are resenting others, praying for them daily, vigorously, and wholeheartedly is guaranteed to alleviate resentment. The other people may or may not change, but we will. Prayer is a terrific way of dealing with people who exercise their ability to irritate us.

When we choose to hold onto unforgiveness, we tend to rationalize. "God knows why I don't forgive the other guy. I was right and he was wrong. Maybe if he calls and apologizes for that thing he said ten years ago, then maybe I will forgive."

I remember one man sitting in front of me at a gathering. I must have given a talk or something and he sought me out. He wanted to make sure that I knew that God knew why he didn't forgive a certain person. He said, "God knows that I don't forgive so-and-so, because he really is a miserable, miserable human being."

No, God doesn't care why we don't forgive. He commands us to forgive. It doesn't matter what our resentment is. We have no choice in the matter except obedience to God or disobedience. We have to make that overture forward. When we are finally free of our unforgiveness, we experience the bricks coming off our back because an unforgiving heart buries us. We see this in the Prodigal Son. If you look at the older brother, poor thing, the weight of the resentment kept him in bondage.

As mentioned, many of us are more willing to forgive others than we are to forgive ourselves.

Forgiving Ourselves

I remember talking to a stewardess who told me that she refused to forgive herself for not seeing her mother before she died. She missed being with her by just a few hours because of a late flight. Her mom lived in another state and the stewardess had just returned home from visiting her mom when she received a call to come back. It's easy for you and I to see that the stewardess was blameless. Nevertheless, this unforgiveness kept her in bondage for many years.

We don't do anyone any justice when we don't forgive ourselves...but we do harm our relationship with Jesus. God already knows our sins. He already knows what we did. In fact, He was there before we did it because He projected our sin from the cross. He said, "Carol Razza – she's going to do this – with that big mouth – she's going to point her finger at someone and say some hurtful words, but I love her enough that I am going to be nailed to this cross anyway." He knows our sins. He forgives our sins. We need to forgive ourselves.

When we start to forgive ourselves, we break through the bondage of slavery. 2 Peter 2:19 tells us, *"For surely anyone is the slave of that by which he has been overcome."* We become slave to that unforgiveness, to that anger, to that rage, to that self-condemnation. We become a slave to it, and we walk in it. We live in it. We're not free. We're tied up.

Our younger son was probably about ten months old and at that age when they're crawling around and trying to climb things like steps. We lived in New York at the time and we had one of these tri-level houses, so any place we went we had to walk up six steps. We were down in our playroom and it was six steps to get up to the main part of the house. Timothy was crawling up these steps and at that time my father-in-law was visiting us for the day. My father-in-law made a statement about something and he wanted to affirm that he was telling the truth, so he said, "You see my grandson – I swear on his legs," and I'll never forget this, "I swear on his legs that I'm telling the truth." Well, I went ballistic and said, "Don't you dare swear on my baby's legs. Swear on your own legs!"

That night, in a dream, God gave me this vision of my late mother-in-law sitting at the end of my bed. She was dressed in what she wore in the casket. I should have jumped out of my skin shaking and trembling and screaming, but instead I listened. She looked at me. She and my father-in-law had been separated for a long time, and she wasn't very pleased with him. So coming from her mouth, what she said meant a lot. She looked at me and said, "Forgive him." Then she startled me by saying, "Stop hating him."

Well, I didn't think I hated him. I just thought that he was bad and I had to be tough with him. I never would have described my feelings using the word, "hate." As far as I was concerned, I was a lover; I didn't hate people. But she said, "Stop hating him and forgive him. All he wants to do is to love his grandchildren and he doesn't know how to do that."

There was truly a miracle that night. I woke up then, not in fear, but in tremendous joy. My husband almost had a stroke because I excitedly woke him up and almost shouted, "Paul, I don't hate your father anymore!" He said, "I didn't know you ever did."

I recognize now that God needed to intervene in that way because it was so miraculous. I didn't have to do anything. It truly was a gift. I felt the difference immediately and experienced for myself what it's like to be in bondage, not know it, and then to be set free.

From here in the perspective of twenty years later, I believe this happened so that God could help me to better understand and serve my brothers and sisters in Christ. Because now I can more clearly see that most of the people I work with have their problems rooted in an unforgiving heart. In fact, probably 60% of my patients suffer from some form of unforgiveness with half of them stuck in unforgiveness towards others and the other half suffering the self-inflicted wound of not forgiving oneself.

From that vision of my mother-in-law to this day, I always try to make the immediate choice to forgive. Maybe it's just selfish because it feels much better but it's the right choice because Jesus calls us to forgive. He commands it.

Forgiveness is an action word. It's not really therapeutic to lay back and issue a blanket statement to the world, "I forgive you." We are forgiving the causes and perpetrators of our hurts. We need to look at our hurts, wrestle with them, and know what we are forgiving as we offer them up to The Lord for healing.

That miracle changed my life and I didn't even know the Lord well then. However, I did allow Him to work in my life. From that point on, some tremendous miracles continued to happened. Paul and I came into a much fuller experience with the Lord, and my father-in-law, before he died, was able to accept the Lord in his life. He was transformed. He was changed. I just know it started that night in that dream and afterwards when I prayed, "Enough is enough. I'm not going to live in unforgiveness anymore."

I never went up to my father-in-law and said, "You know I hated you once." I never did that because that would have hurt him. But my spirit, my relationship with God, and my relationship with others all changed when God removed the bitterness of unforgiveness from my heart.

We need to allow God to reveal those parts of our lives where we may be harboring unforgiveness. When those experiences start to surface, know that God is surfacing it so that we can be free from it. He is not putting it in front of our faces to cause us more suffering.

I remember a number of years ago, there was a woman in Dallas who was car-jacked and brutally stabbed, raped, sodomized, and left for dead. She didn't die, but she was blinded. I heard her interviewed on the radio a year or two after the horrible incident, and the interviewer asked her how she had survived with her life so radically changed.

He said, "You must hate this man." The man was in prison.

She said, "No. In fact, I have forgiven him and I went to prison to tell him that."

The interviewer said, "How could you do that?"

She said, "Well, he took that one night away from me, and I wouldn't give him anymore of my life."

Freedom comes in forgiving ourselves and in forgiving others.

I think the best model for us in offering forgiveness is the Blessed Virgin. I look at the experience she went through and I say to myself, "How dare I ever not want to forgive someone!" She saw her son rejected, spit upon, tortured, scorned, and yet she chose to forgive Peter and the apostles. Peter denied him and the apostles fled but she chose to forgive them. This is a profound lesson for us.

As Christians, we are not experiencing the fullness of our God because we are not doing the things we need to do. God is doing His part. He keeps pouring down His mercy, pouring down His forgiveness. Yet we create umbrellas and hide under them. We're not receiving it fully. His grace is all around us, but it is not penetrating who we are and freeing us from that deep down soul sickness that infects too many Christians.

We want to make this moment in time different. Everyday I pray, "Lord, I don't want to do things the same as I did yesterday. I want to change and to grow. Teach me. Whatever I did yesterday, that wasn't totally embracing you, show me and teach me. I want to grow to know grace like a fish knows water.

In 2 Corinthians 3:17 *"So whoever is in Christ is a new creation. The old things have passed away. Behold, new things have come."*

Listen closely to that soft voice within as our Father tells us we are forgiven. We need to feel it. Meditation is a sublime form of listening; we need to listen for forgiveness.

We have such a beautiful parable that supports us in the whole area of forgiveness in the Prodigal Son. We know the story. Look at the difference in what a forgiving and repentant heart looks like compared to an unforgiving heart. Which of the characters do you identify with? Compare the father's joyous forgiveness compared to the older son's bitter unforgiveness and the prodigal son's repentance.

When couples come in for counseling, the first thing I ask them to do is write a letter to their partner asking forgiveness for something that God puts on their heart that they've done to their spouse. It can be anything. I say, "Whatever God reveals to you, write that." This is not a 'but' letter. It's not, 'I was so nasty and I yelled at you, <u>but</u> I only did it because you came home drunk' " No, not that! Take responsibility and assume a repentant heart.

Look at the forgiving heart of the prodigal son's father, which really allows us to see that unexpected forgiveness that our God gives us. He had a courageous love. He ran out to embrace him. He defied all the norms at that time. This is a wonderful example of a forgiving heart.

When others seek forgiveness from us, we need to run to them, embrace them, to shower them with the same gracious mercy that our Father shows us.

I remember praying over a woman from our prayer community. She came to a conference and came up to me and to two other people for prayer. I had this real sense that she wasn't forgiving someone. So I looked at her and I said, "You're holding on to someone and it's a female. Who is it?" She looked me straight in the eye and said, "You."

As soon as she said it, God put on my heart, "Just say you're sorry." I didn't know what she was going to say. "Just say you're sorry." So I said, "What did I do?" I really didn't know what it was all about. She said, "Two years ago, I was in the hospital and you never came to see me." Well, I said to her, "I'm just so sorry."

I didn't say, "Two years ago, wow, I was going through such horrible problems at that time; I mean I didn't even know where I was, let alone where you were." I really didn't even remember that she had been in the hospital. But I didn't say any of that. I just said, "I'm sorry."

Well, with that, I saw scales just drop off this woman. I was grateful that God put on my heart first, "Just say you're sorry," because I would have wanted to jump in there and give some very good excuses. That would have been my approach, but He said, "Just say you're sorry." "Just say you're sorry."

A forgiving heart is an extension of God's mercy and it is a celebration of repentance. The father in the prodigal son story had a party just like God celebrates every time we forgive ourselves for things that we are still holding onto. Our spirit needs to be one of celebration. We need to walk closer to holiness and conversion, and the only way we do that is to get rid of the baggage that we've carried for so long.

Some people aren't forgiving themselves for things they've done as kids, as teenagers. Well, how dare us — how dare us condemn those little babies! We're different people today! We need to say, "Oh, wow, I did that? Poor thing. I must have been so lost or in so much pain." But we still condemn ourselves. It's time to give that up. The enemy wants us to stay stuck with our baggage, away from God and away from grace. We obey the enemy when we say, "Okay, I'll stay stuck. I'll keep beating myself up." We say yes to toxic unforgiveness. It's time to say yes to God!

Let's look further at the unforgiving heart. Sometimes we put that wall up and say, "Oh, I can't do it." Consider the woman I spoke of earlier who contemplated suicide after her abortion. She was saying "no" to God. She was saying, "You may have forgiven me. Scripture says you forgive people. But I can't forgive myself."

She refused to forgive herself and instead closed herself off from grace and hardened her heart. Look at the prodigal son's older brother; he had an unforgiving heart. He felt so justified. He was great at rationalization. He became cold. He would not celebrate. He was going to walk past that party. "Hey, my father never did that for me."

How many times have we said things like that? We get so petty sometimes. We get jealous of our neighbors or brothers and whine to ourselves, "Poor me. I am a good and deserving person and I even go to church. How come I didn't get that and they did?"

It never occurs to us to celebrate with them. We can't celebrate if our hearts are hardened. We just don't have it within us. We are going to have it now, though, because we are asking God to help us uncover anything that is keeping us from forgiveness and trust.

I know, without a shadow of a doubt, that He calls us together and He calls us by name. Here you are reading about unforgiveness. You are reading this for a reason. Is it an accident or part of His plan to bring you to wholeness? If reading this chapter has dredged up issues of unforgiveness that you are ready to give up, then get rid of that umbrella that blocks you from grace. Rip it up! Tear it! Stamp on it! Get wet! Get wet with God's love! Love, rain on me! When is the last time you ran in the rain? Take a risk and lower the shields.

Choosing forgiveness means, "I am obedient to you, Lord. I have chosen life in you." We are going to continue to pray that God reveals the blocks that stop us from total and complete forgiveness, from making that choice each day to say, "Yes, Lord, I believe in You so much that whatever You call me to do, I'm going to do. I'm going to trust You."

"Lord, I believe that You and You alone are the God of forgiveness. Lord, I pray that as we continue through this book, You continue to reveal to us those areas of unforgiveness that we still harbor in our heart. Very often when things are revealed to us, we start to condemn ourselves because of it. So Lord, let us know that it is You. Let us know that You are not about condemnation. You are about healing and restoration. We

129

pray, Lord, that we are restored to what You created us to be in the womb. Reveal to us our giftedness and the direction that You want us to take as whole and healed and healthy believers. In Your son, Jesus Christ, we pray. Amen.

Chapter 10

Get Out of the Boat

I used to secretly wonder why the apostles seemed to have all the same frailties that we modern Christians suffer. How could they doubt when they walked, talked, and lived with Jesus Christ? How could they experience fear with Jesus performing miracles right before their very eyes? I suppose that I thought that my faith would be perfect if only I walked, talked, and lived with Jesus like the apostles did.

Mathew 14:28 *"Lord, if it is Thou, bid me come to thee over the water. And He said, "Come."*

One of my favorite bible stories is when Jesus walked on the water and Peter wanted so badly to join him. It was the night that the apostles had witnessed the miracle of the loaves and fishes. Can you imagine how dramatic and attractive Jesus looked to those in the boat as He walked on the water? I identify with Peter so much because, like him, I am weak. But like him, I am so attracted to Jesus that I want to walk with him.

Walking with Jesus involves risk. It's just as true today as it was in the time of the apostles. One has to have more faith than fear. To walk with Jesus involves getting out of a perfectly safe and comfortable little boat. It involves a leap of faith.

How many of us are frozen in fear or apathy? Peter wasn't frozen. He got out of the boat and began to walk on the water, moving toward Jesus. However, when he perceived how strong the wind was, becoming frightened, he began to sink and cry out, "Lord, save me!" Jesus at once stretched out his hand and caught him. "*How little faith you have*", he exclaimed, "*Why did you doubt?*" Once they had climbed into the boat, the wind died down. Those who were in the boat saw that even the winds and the seas obeyed Jesus and declared, "Beyond doubt you are the Son of God."

Are you willing to come out of the boat or do you prefer to try to hide behind the little walls and blocks that you have built for yourself? Are you willing to come out of the boat right here, right now? To surrender your agenda and give it up to the Lord? Are you willing to open up that Pandora's Box that maybe has been locked up for a long time? Are you willing to put the rifles down? Are you willing to take the required but always uncomfortable leap of faith it takes to walk with Jesus?

Very often during retreats and in counseling I hear people say, "I've found some blocks; I didn't even know I had them." Are we willing to leave them at the foot of the cross? Are we willing to follow Him no matter what the cost, at any cost? Tough questions.

Those were tough questions for Peter but that night he had the willingness to follow Jesus. He made a decision and he acted on it. He didn't cower in the boat. He didn't hide there in his comfortable seat and pretend not to see Jesus out there beckoning. Peter took the leap of faith and stepped out of the boat.

I cannot tell you how important this story is to me. The rock upon which Christ eventually built his church started to sink in fear only steps into his walk. Here was Jesus, right in front of him, but all it took was for some wind and waves to kick up, and Peter the human starts to doubt and sink. The rock upon which Christ would build his church apparently has the very same petty fears and doubts that I tend to have when the winds and seas of life kick me around.

The response of Jesus to Peter's fear gives me so much hope. Instead of letting Peter drown in his fear, instead of kicking Peter out of the select, Christ extended a loving and helpful hand. Like a loving father helping a toddler who has tripped, Jesus immediately brought Peter to safety and gently reminded him to improve his faith. Jesus perfectly forgave Peter for his human frailties and extended a helping hand.

Even after we make a decision to accept Jesus Christ as our Savior, very often when the storms kick up in our lives we don't have the faith to stand up there and to continue to walk. I don't think Peter was much different than the rest of us. But he did have enough faith to do the impossible.... he walked on water. He took a risk by stepping towards God, and it turned out to be an important part of his spiritual journey. Will we take the risk and step out from behind our blocks towards God's grace?

The part I really like is that, even though Peter was full of flaws, doubts, and fears...God loved him unconditionally. Even though Peter sank in doubt, and later even denied knowing Jesus, God didn't abandon Peter but invested grace in him instead.

We are all on different parts of our faith journey. We all have a story, or many stories, about how we "walked on water" when we were first baptized in the Spirit. Don't tell my neighbors this, but I used to go into the local hospital and walk down the hallways laying hands on the doors praying for the people inside. I didn't know who they were or what was going on; I was just believing that they would be healed. I felt so strongly that God had called me and would reveal different healings to me. I felt like Peter must have felt when he walked on the water.

Then, I went through a dry time and all of a sudden it was, "Whoa - where is God now?" Where is this great gift of the Spirit and the excitement I felt. And I started to sink very much like Peter.

Peter cried out, "Lord, save me!" I followed his example and cried out, "Help, I don't know what's happening." But the Lord had work to do with me. He wasn't ready for me to stop learning yet even though it felt like I was sinking. When my time in the spiritual desert got so bad that I cried out, "Help!" He immediately reached out His hand as He did with Peter and pulled me into the boat. I'm very grateful for that.

I believe we all have similar stories, those times when we were walking on water and saying, "Wow, Jesus is great, Amen, Hallelujah!" Then, boom, all of a sudden fear creeps in and the Lord pulled us in. The point is that, no matter where we are in our journey, the hand of Jesus is *always* there for the asking. If we are still cowering in the boat afraid to come out, we need to remember that trying to hide from Jesus is the saddest thing we could possibly do to ourselves.

The last few chapters have talked about not fearing what's going on inside and fearlessly opening yourself up to the Lord for healing. For those of you to whom God already started revealing things, you're recognizing that He's revealing them without condemnation. He's revealing them so that you can be joyous and free.

He will continue to show all of us those areas that we still haven't attended to in our life. Instead of fearing His condemnation, we should expect his helping hand. To walk in courage and strength and trust we must allow the Lord's grace to penetrate what's still locked up and hidden away. Whatever silly belief systems we have adopted that need to be blown apart, ask for grace and help. We are not alone. We all, at one time or another, adopt belief systems that are simply not true.

Any area in our heart that still remains broken, we need only ask His healing grace. For souls that are still damaged, ask Him to nurture and fill them with glorious grace. Let Him handle our ancestral tree that needs to be healed. Let Him reconcile those areas of unforgiveness and distrust. Let faith wash out the bitter fears. Let hope overcome despair.

Get Out of the Boat Today...Here's How

What an order! How do we take the first step out of the boat? I believe it starts in the head.

We have the information. We know the Scriptures. I think it starts in the mind but it can't stay there. We need to continue to fill our minds with the knowledge of His word. The truth of Romans 8:35, *"Who shall separate us from the love of Christ? Shall tribulation or distress or persecution or famine or nakedness or peril or the sword?"* We need to know that nothing can separate us from Him as we take the next step.

Romans 8:28, *"And we know that God causes all things to work together for good to those who love God, to those who are called according to His purpose."*

We have been called according to His purpose. I think this is the part that we sometimes forget. We hear *"I'm called"*, and we kind of believe it, but called *"according to His purpose?"* When we see things not going just perfectly, according to our own worldly standards of perfection, we need to recognize it's not about our purpose, it's about His. Whatever that might be.

I Peter 2:9, *"But you are a chosen race, a royal priesthood, a holy nation, a people for God's own possession, that you may proclaim the excellence of Him who has called you out of darkness into His marvelous light."* Am I living in His marvelous light?

Isaiah 43:16, *"Fear not for I have redeemed you. I have called you by name. You are mine."*

Fill your head constantly with these Scriptures that build up our spirit, that tell us the truth.

Perhaps many of you will remember a movie from a few years ago called Simon Burch. Simon Burch was a dwarfish boy. Because of some disease he hadn't grown to full size and his life expectancy wasn't long. He believed throughout his life, in his heart of hearts, that he had an important purpose. He told everyone that God created him for a purpose. Of course, he was right because we are all created for a purpose.

Simon had a keen sense of mission. No one could stop him from believing in his mission. In one scene he stands up in church and he tells the congregation how he was created for a grand and wonderful purpose. The minister tells him to sit down, "I'm the preacher here."

Simon was right. He is on a school bus full of children and the bus skids off an icy road and plunges into a freezing lake. While the other older kids selfishly scrambled to safety, Simon bravely stayed behind, broke a window, and saved perhaps a dozen little kids who would have drowned. He died as a result.

When I saw the movie, I thought, "What a true story." Whoever wrote that wrote truth. We are all called according to His purpose.

Simon Burch isn't the only one with a God-mission. It's true for each and every one of us. The closest we can possibly be to truly achieving peace and happiness in this life is during those times when we can put aside our egos and make a decision to align our will with God's will for us. That deep soul satisfaction we all want so badly is not something we can go out and get, rather, it comes only as a byproduct of turning our will over to God. We need to ask Him now what His will for us might be.

We can't think in terms of grandiosity and ego. Perhaps God's will for you is to be a humble servant instead of winning the lottery. Jesus Christ, a humble carpenter born in a barn is our example. How can we serve God by humbly and compassionately helping the people that He places in our lives? Don't worry about exactly what your mission is; rather concentrate on what He wants you to do today. Ask for courage to do the next right thing. Use the Prayer of St. Francis as your guide.

Each and every one of us is called. We have <u>not</u> been called to live trapped on a boat named fear, distrust, soul sickness, heartache or unforgiveness. Jesus calls us to Him. The normal human reaction is to want to stay in the boat, hide in the boat, because the devil tells us it's safe and dry there. But the boat is our prison. Our fate is sealed and our misery is guaranteed if we choose to stay stuck and hide. We have free will. If we're going to follow Jesus and step out of the boat, we need to remember that we're going to step towards something. We are stepping towards freedom and salvation. We need to know, know without a shadow of a doubt, that God has a wonderful plan of joy and freedom for us. This is truth.

It needs to start in our minds. We have to stop believing the lie. In our hearts and minds, we know it's a lie that hiding in our defects will make us happy. We tend to think in negative terms of "giving up" our wonderful warm and safe places just like an alcoholic doesn't want to "give up" his or her precious bottle. They don't want to take a loss. But you and I can dispassionately see that what the alcoholic is really "giving up" is a life of addiction, misery, hangovers, broken families, lost jobs, and liver damage. It's only an illusion that he or she is "giving up" something comfortable and safe...like our seats on the boat.

John 4:18, *"There is no fear in love. But perfect love casts out all fear."*

If fear is blocking you from stepping out of the boat, from taking that plunge... start by saying, "Yes Lord, I know that You are here. You invited me here, to

138

this crossroads, and I want You to reveal it all. I want to know what it is that's still keeping me blocked from You. Yes, Lord I believe."

A friend of mine who leads music for many of the retreats I direct, Dennis Garrity, writes a lot of wonderful inspirational songs. My favorite line from one of the songs is, "Yes Lord, I Believe; You are the one Who came from Heaven. I'll follow where You lead, I'll follow where You lead."

That's what we need to say to Him right now. "Yes, Lord, I believe and I want to follow where You lead. I'm not going to be in control anymore. I'm not controlling the ship. I'm giving up control to You." It's a well-known spiritual paradox that the only way to win is to surrender. The only way to be free, to become unshackled from the bondage of our petty fears and egos…is to hand it all over to the Lord and say, "Yes, Lord, I am here and I humbly and gratefully accept your invitation to follow." Most of us haven't yet lived in the freedom that comes with this kind of surrender.

I remember a student of mine in one of the college psychology courses I taught. She had a history of abuse in her family. I asked her to go to the back of the Bible and read the letters of John. I recommended that she read them in a personal way, like God is talking directly to her. She said, "I haven't read the Bible since I was a little girl," and I said it didn't matter. You can read it as a big girl. She did and in the process of reading it she would call every couple of days. The Lord put it in my heart to tell her to read it, read it and read it again. She would call every few days sobbing how she never realized how much God loved her and that she didn't have to hold onto the fears that she'd been holding onto for so long. She was totally transformed by the Word of God.

That kind of transformation needs to happen to us every time we open the Good Book. We need to be totally engaged, never get bored with what He has to say to us because He loves us so much.

We need to take down the umbrella. You know how sometimes the wind catches it and it flies up? We have to hope that happens with our umbrellas that are blocking the grace that God is shedding on us. We want to turn the knowledge and wisdom from the Word into empowerment. We have to stop believing the lies and get truth into our heads. That's where you start…but sometimes that's where people stop. We want to crack open the door and let God's empowerment completely flood our hearts, minds, souls, and every crevice of our lives.

It's not enough if it just stays in our minds. It has to change us. We want to know the truth of God's Word. We want to see the world through the eyes of the prophet. We don't want to see it through our flesh eyes anymore. So we're not going to fearfully look at our situation. We want to say, "Lord allow me to see through the eyes of the prophet, so I can see beyond what I'm going through. Whether it's problems in my marriage, problems with my children or grandchildren, work, my faith, whatever it might be - Lord give me the eyes to see beyond it."

We get too stuck in the trees and we can't see the forest. We can't step out of the boat if we're only looking at the dangerous sea. We can't falter or we'll sink. We have to look straight in His eyes. Never, never loose touch with those eyes. To me, His eyes on the cross are incredible. If we could focus on His eyes just before He says, "It is finished," we have it made. We don't have to sink. Let them pierce our soul, our inner being. Then we can get out of the boat. We can't be fearful anymore when that happens.

We are never as close to God as we are when we are in trouble. As Peter sunk, Jesus was right there with His outstretched hand. When the trial comes and our brokenness is so apparent, we know that He is strong in our weakness. When tribulation comes, a healthy mental attitude says, "This is a time to embrace." We don't have to like it. I don't think any of us ever enjoy trial no matter how deeply we know that the Lord is using the occasion for good purpose.

When in the midst of trial, we can say, "Okay Lord, it's a time for You to carry me." He carries us. The famous poem, Footprints, reflects truth. We get so close we can feel Him breathe. We know that he is holding us through the trail. We can feel His strength. We can relax and trust Him completely. He is Abba.

Our God never leaves us. Philippians 4:11-13, says, *"Not that I speak from want, for I have learned to be content in whatever circumstances I am. I know how to get along with humble means and I also know how to live in prosperity. In any and every circumstance I have learned the secret of being filled and going hungry. Both of having abundance and suffering need. I can do all things through Him who strengthens me."*

It's worth repeating, "*I can do all things through Him who strengthens me.*" These are not just words, they are truth. Anyone who has embraced these words can give witness to that truth.

The mistake that we make is when we say, "Oh Lord I do believe you're going to heal me," and then we live in the fear of it not happening. Faith and hope move mountains. Fear and despair keep us in the boat.

For example, your little children might come to you and say, "I know the circus is coming, I want to go, are we going to go?" We might reply, "Not tonight, but Saturday." Well, the kids are so excited because they know Saturday will come and they tell all their friends. Jesus tells us we have to be childlike. When God tells us in Scripture that He hears us and will heal us, we can know it and embrace it and walk in the understanding of that guarantee. Just like the kids who know they are going to the circus, we can say the same thing, "Hey, Saturday my God is healing me completely. He's nourishing my soul. He's healing my distrust and my unforgiveness. He's healing my fears because that's what He says."

We don't know how God will manifest that healing. We tend to think "healing" means "having it MY way." But in reality, His way is much better. We want Him to heal us, we ask Him to heal us, and we have a written guarantee that Saturday is going to come. He never, ever leaves us. There's always a purpose in trial. It's always going to bring us to a higher place. Every problem that I have faced and endured as a Christian, has strengthened me, helped me grow, and therefore made me more able to serve. He is preparing us, molding us, training us for our missions. No pain, no gain.

I Peter 1:3-4, *"Blessed be the God and Father of our Lord Jesus Christ, Who according to His great mercy has caused us to be born again to a living hope through the resurrection of Jesus Christ from the dead to obtain an inheritance which is imperishable and undefiled and will not fade away."*

Did you grasp those words? Read them again.... *"to obtain an inheritance which is imperishable and undefiled and will not fade away."* It doesn't fade away when we're going through bad times. It doesn't fade away when were anxious or in debt or in poor health. It doesn't fade away when I don't feel God. It never fades away.

One cannot simultaneously experience gratitude and depression. Today is a time to rejoice. It doesn't matter what trials we are going through. Our God says that He is changing us and empowering us and He is lovingly with us every step of the way.

Praise God - He wants His children to trust Him. He wants to love us and make us whole. That's all He wants to do, but we have to trust Him. We look within and see what's blocking us from The Light.

We need to step out of the boat. We can't focus anymore on the problems. We need to focus on the glory of God. We will see the glory of God through the cross. We won't see it any other way. We have to focus on it and know that it's coming.

When you finish this chapter, take a few quiet moments with The Lord. Let tonight be a personal Pentecost for you and again tomorrow and the next day again. Peter had that Pentecost that grew him up into the spiritual giant that he became. Every day we need to say, "Lord, please do it again. I want more Lord, I want more of Your Spirit and more of Your grace. I want to be the best I can in You."

Jeremiah 33:3, *"Call to me and I will answer you and I will tell you great and mighty things which you do not know."*

All He asks for is our call. If we just call Him, He's going to tell us all these things we don't even know. Call to Him now. *"Lord, tell me. I want to know these great and mighty things."*

The Lord put a Scripture on my heart and I want to use it in closing this chapter. It's Isaiah 43:18, *"Do not call to mind the former things or ponder things of the past. Behold I will do something new. Now it will spring forth. Will you not be aware of it? I will even make a roadway in the wilderness, rivers in the desert."*

If our lives look like a wilderness, God right now is making a roadway. He's running mighty rivers to the dry part of our lives to quench our spirits, to quench the emptiness in our souls. Let's be open to that and take the risk. It's Abba and He is extending His helping hand and coaxing us out of bondage.

Chapter 11

Let His Light Shine

Luke 8:16 - *"Now no one, after lighting a lamp, covers it over with a container or puts it under a bed. But he puts it on a lamp stand in order that those who come in may see the light"*.

Let His Light shine. Well, we're out of the boat, right? We want to make sure that, as we walk across the water in faith and grace, people see us so brightly that it allows them to get out of their boats as well.

How do we do that? That's the big question. How do we continue to let our light shine through the different obstacles that come our way?

The first thing to remember is that it is crucially important for us to continue to pray, *"Lord, keep searching me. Let me be right out there with you. Let me be so intimate with you that when something starts to surface that I don't want to see, that you let me see it so that I can get rid of it, so I can face it and deal with it and move on."*

Read 2 Corinthians 7, starting around verse 8. This was the second letter to the Corinthians. In the first one Paul really slammed them. They were doing a lot of things that needed to be corrected. In this particular couple of verses, he said, and I'll paraphrase *"You know, if I saddened you by my first letter, good! If it brought you to that point of godly repentance, then great!"*

Paul says that a godly repentance will immediately turn us around. We repent and we know that we're forgiven and we get on with our lives. Compare this to a worldly sadness when we just beat ourselves up.

Pray

What we want to do is to continue to pray and ask God to reveal things and when He does, if there are areas that we need to repent of, we repent, and get on with things – rather than staying stuck. We really need to ask God to continue to open up those areas of our heart and of our mind that need to be revealed..

Confess

We need to confess any unconfessed sin. I feel particularly blessed because the Catholic Church celebrates the sacraments. The Sacrament of Reconciliation is beautiful. I experience God's grace in such a powerful way. Whether in a sacramental setting or not, confessing our sins is a vehicle to holiness. The twelve steps of recovery include a very important step involving confession of our sins to ourselves, to another human being, and to God.

Reconcile

We need to reconcile with those that we have hurt. If God has put someone on our hearts that we need to reconcile with, that we've caused damage to, then do it! Life is too short to hold onto things and stubbornly say, "No, I'm not going to do it." If someone has hurt us, we can forgive him or her. If there is no reconciliation because the other person doesn't want to come into that reconciliation, we need to at least attempt reconciliation.

Bondage of Lies
We need to ask God each day to probe us and reveal to us any untruth that we've embraced. We embrace lies all the time without even realizing it. The Holy Spirit has that very fine surgeon's instrument that cuts away at lies and sets us free. Let's allow the Holy Spirit to do that work instead of beating ourselves to death with a club. We want Him to do it, so that He can reveal the lies that damage us and block the Son's Light.

Soul
Look at the soul. It's solar-powered which means that we have to keep refilling it with God's Light. Your soul nourishes you and God nourishes it. One of the greatest joyful experiences in life is knowing that we are loved by God Almighty. If we don't know it in every cell of our body, then we need to examine the state of our souls. Ask God each day to continue to heal your soul and fill it with grace. Many of the Psalms can be helpful. Many of them help us pray for restoration and soul healing.

Affirmation
We also need to affirm ourselves by saying things like, "I am accepted. I am loved. I am called to live in the power of the Lord, in the love of the Lord. He calls me precious. Nothing I can do today will make God love me more and no sin or failure will make God love me less – He just loves." I know we say those things, but we don't always act accordingly. I hear people all the time say, "I

know that God always forgives me," yet they don't live as if they are forgiven people.

Rumford, in his book <u>Soul Shaping</u>, says, "When we live our lives expecting and depending upon the undeserved grace of God's love, we find that its clear, fresh waters bubble up at the most unexpected times, reminding us that we are royal children. When someone tries to attack our integrity, God's love fills us with confidence. When we would normally shrink from responsibility, God's love fills us with assurance. God's love gives us a moment of joy in the midst of mundane duty, washing away the dirt of life in this dusty world. A vital life is rooted in grace. No other soil will bear lasting fruit."

Ah, isn't that so true? When our souls are healed and whole, we can be in any situation and we get the strength we need to deal with whatever we need to deal with in that moment. Our light will never go out if we continue to nurture our soul. A healthy soul will bring forth fruitfulness in our faith experience.

Hope
Despair is the exact opposite of hope. Guess which one feels better. Attitude is a choice. Hope is the feeling that The Lord is always there and has a plan for you that is more joyous and fulfilling than your wildest dreams. It's bone deep knowledge that His hand is there to help us through whatever's going on in my life. It means knowing in our hearts that God isn't going to allow anything to happen in our lives that we can't handle. Hope is the certainty of knowing that we are never going to be alone and the closer to the Lord we are, the better for both us and for everyone who comes into contact with us.

With an attitude of hope, we can see the glory of each day no matter what is going on in our life. I think we get so caught up sometimes and get so blindsided by the problems, that we miss the glory of the day. When our souls are healthy, we see the glory of His plan in each minute of each day. We are not saints. We don't have to like it. We can be angry. We can be hurt. But we never lose site of the big picture where our Daddy is right beside us every step of the way.

Expectant Spirit

An expectant spirit is fueled from within. We are realistic and optimistic at the same time. I remember when our older son was only about eight years old. Our boys used to go to an equestrian camp and they were in the pickup truck going from one place to another. Paulie, our older son, said that a song came on the radio that he was very unhappy with; he said it upset his spirit. So I said, "So what did you do? Did you tell Casey to change the station?" He said, "No, Mom, I just prayed. I knew that God would take care of it. And He did. Casey changed it." It is this kind of faith, childlike faith, with which we have to approach life. We have to remember to look at life through the eyes of a prophet. "Lord, give me the eyes of a prophet to look past my momentary situation.

Resilience

A healthy soul brings with it resilience and patience, the ability to recover from misfortune or to adjust to change. This doesn't mean that we are naive. We just know in our heart of hearts that God has a plan. A number of people have told me that God put a vision or plan on their heart that didn't actually come to fullness until years and years and years later. We need to have that resilience to wait for God's plan to unfold.

149

Over twenty years ago my husband and I were at a conference where a wonderful, women of God spoke. I connected with her right away, I just loved her. Afterwards, she didn't even know who I was, and I went up and kissed her and introduced myself.

During the conference, my husband Paul looked at me and said, "Someday, I'm going to see you up there speaking." So I said, "What will I say? In time, God started to bring all that to fullness. We need to look for His plan for us. We need to be willing and obedient to it. It could take fifteen or twenty years or more, but it happens. Whatever He has put on our heart, know that He is going to give us the power and grace to get there. We don't have to micromanage it, just try to make prayerful daily decisions and be open to His will for us on a daily basis.

Several years ago, I remember we were planning to go to the Holy Lands. My dad had died and we were taking care of my mom who had a series of strokes. We were emotionally exhausted. Right after we made reservations for the trip, my mom died. At the time I was working on my doctorate, and was only allowed to miss one class per course. The death of my mom and the first day of the Holy Land trip both fell on days that would have taken me away from class.

The boys and Paul prayed for me when I went in to speak to the director of the program. I said, "You know, I really need this trip. I need to get away. Is there any way that we can bend the rules?" He said, "No. I give you credit; I don't know how you made it so far. But, I really can't. But what I can do for you is I could allow you to miss the class and then retake the course again. So, you will graduate a year later but you will be able to go to the Holy Lands."

I looked at him and I said, "I would rather take glass and crush it in my eyes than be in this program for another year." I got in the car and put on praise music for the hour-long drive back to my house. I have this little Miata with the top down, and I'm praising the Lord, shouting. Two young men at a light looked at me and thought I was a lunatic. But I didn't care; I just kept praising the Lord, thanking Him.

The trip to the Holy land was led by a spiritual director that I wanted to get to know better, the women that years prior inspired the comment from Paul. Her name is Babsie and I really wanted to get to know her better because she strikes me as such a Godly woman.

So, I'm driving and praising the Lord, and my heart was being lifted - just a little bit at a time, because I had really wanted to go. By the time I got home, the Lord had put on my heart, "I have something better for you." I walked into the house and I must have looked as joyous as I felt. Paul was on the phone with boys and looked at me and he told our sons, "Mom's home. It looks like we're going!" I said, "No, God has something better for us."

The reality was that God did have something better for us. Within months, we had Babsie at our home as a houseguest and we became close friends. Later she put organized a pilgrimage with Fr. Michael Moses and only twenty of us went and so it was very beautiful. God only gives us what's best for us. Even though I had to wait, it came in His time. I think sometimes we bellyache so much that we miss the glory of the moment. We need to let our light shine in patience and resilience

Compassion

We have to access compassion for others. Sometimes it is dead in us. For me, the model of compassion is Mother Theresa. She exemplified compassion for others and we have to look for that in ourselves. Compassion is the vital sign of a healthy soul. If we've lost our compassion for others, our soul is telling us something. A by-product of loving God is our love for other people. If this is not happening, then something must be blocking us from the Son. Are we doing something to prevent our full and complete exposure to God's grace? Our service to others, in love and compassion is an expression of our salvation. Too often we miss the needy because we are too busy giving lip service to the Lord. There are so many issues of social justice that would be reconciled if we as Christians would actively reach out in compassion to those in need.

Zeal

True zeal is not just enthusiasm. It is energy, a power, and a commitment to one another and to Jesus. Paul describes this in 2 Corinthians, "For the love of Christ controls me." That's what zeal is – being controlled by the love of Christ. We are so overwhelmed with His love that it pours out. We're so overwhelmed that we have to act on it. A healthy soul brings zeal.

Integrity

Integrity is a sign of the fruit of the Spirit. What I say and what I do are the same. We become responsible. We walk the walk. If we are going to walk around saying, "Praise you, Jesus! Alleluia!" then we better act that way in all situations. How many people do you think go to church on Sunday and cheat on their taxes and on their spouses? I don't think God gives us too much room. I really don't. I think this is where we fall short as believers. This is where we have to encourage one another and admonish one another.

My husband told me a story the other day about driving to work in heavy traffic. There was a woman behind him sitting on her horn – beeping, beeping, beeping, beeping, but he couldn't move. Well, when she finally had room to pass him, the car had a Christian fish decal and the rearview mirror had rosary beads hanging. The driver gave him a "salute" as she passed. Ouch! Being Christian is a 24/7 proposition and we have to walk a principled walk. We don't have to be saints, but "doing the next right thing" is a habit made easier when we allow God to nourish our soul.

Gratitude

There is an expression in AA that says that you can't feel gratitude and depression at the same time. I am not talking about clinical depression but self-pity. Making a gratitude list is a good way to put things in perspective.

God built us with free will. It's central to His plan. Gratitude is a choice we make. We get to choose whether the glass if half full or half empty. We get to choose whether we are going to bask in God's Light or whether we are going to hide in fear and self-pity. An attitude of gratitude is something that you choose...not so much something that just happens to us when things are going well.

I'm grateful every day because God loves me, because He calls me His beloved, and because I'm redeemed. I was bought for a high price. What else could be more important? Nothing! There is nothing that holds a candle to the Good News. If we are not feeling gratitude, please don't condemn yourself. Just say, "Lord, heal my soul. I want a healthy, healthy soul, so that I can be a light to this hurting world." Gratitude is an action word.

Take Action.

The road to hell is paved with good intentions. I used to think that my good intentions were worth maybe half credit on judgment day. The bottom line is God gives each of us the strength and the power to carry out His will for us. It's not about intentions, it's about actions.

I meet people on a daily basis who say, "I'm trying so hard to behave a certain way." Don't try to behave anymore. Try to love Him more. Let Him love you more. Receive His love more. Give Him your heart. Surrender. Don't try. Do.

When people come into therapy, I can give them techniques. For example, I can give couples techniques to help them to behave better. I'll probably frustrate the life out of them unless they change their hearts. I can't change their hearts. Everything I do and say is to encourage them to ask God to change their hearts.

Action! Think about when you do things out of duty and when you do things out of love- two completely different motives. If I do things out of duty, I don't always have that zeal and excitement. But if I do things out of love, there's a passion there. That's the difference between trying and doing.

I want to leave you with two scriptures:

Jesus clearly tells the apostles in John 16:7-8 – *"If I fail to go, the Paraclete will never come to you; whereas*

154

if I go, I will send him to you. When He comes, He will prove the world wrong about sin, about justice, about condemnation."

John 14:15-17 – *"If you love me and obey the commandments I give to you, I will ask the Father and He will give you another Paraclete, to be with you always, the Spirit of truth, whom the world cannot accept, since it neither sees him nor recognizes him. But you can recognize Him because He remains with you and will be within you."*

The Son hasn't left us orphaned. God gives us all the solar power we need, and more, to get our jobs done during our short mission here on earth. We are a community of Light. When you put this book down... whether you are in bed, on a subway train, or under an umbrella at the beach... remember that God's grace freely pours down all around you. God chose you from the womb. He loves you and His grace is the only thing that will fill your inside and make you fulfilled, joyous, and free.

So the next time you catch yourself building little blocks between you and the Son....Sonblocks.... throw them away and come back to The Light. It's always shining. God blesses you every day. You are never, ever alone!

About the Authors

Dr. Carol Razza (Ed.D.) is a licensed family therapist of 20 years with a thriving family counseling practice in Wellington, Florida. Dr. Razza is very active and well known both in Catholic and Protestant Women's communities and she speaks at dozens of retreats, seminars, and conferences around the country and internationally each year. She has led pilgrimages to Lourdes, the Holy Land, and is active in ministries and relief efforts in Central America and the Caribbean. Dr. Razza is currently an adjunct professor at St. Vincent De Paul Catholic seminary and is Founder of The Ecumenical Women's Prayer Group and the Catholic Women's Prayer Group. Happily married to husband Paul for some 30 years, they have two children, Paul and Timothy.

Denis Eirikis is very active in the recovery community and is a frequent public speaker and award-winning freelance writer. He and his wife own Clear Light Communications Inc., a publishing, marketing and public relations firm that works with a variety of major nonprofit organizations and corporations. Mr. Eirikis has a B.A. from St Thomas University, has served as a Commissioned US Coast Guard Officer, worked in some 46 countries as an oil company executive, and is happily married for 17 years to Leonor. They live in Royal Palm Beach, FL with their three children: Mark, Steven, and Juliet Marie. He found the Lord during a near death experience in 1987.

Speaking Engagements

Dr. Razza has a very active retreat and seminar ministry. If you would like to inquire about speaking to your organization, please contact her office directly at 561/795-5724. If you would like to learn more about her upcoming retreat schedule, please check out www.clearlightcoms.com/carolrazza

Reflecting the Light

The co-authors enthusiastically invite comments from readers. We especially want to know whether you found this book useful in your journey and whether it helped you uncover anything that was blocking you from the fullness in Christ. Any and all of your anecdotes, comments, or suggestions are welcome. Please write to
Attn: SONBLOCK
c/o Clear Light Communications Inc.
254 Las Palmas Street
Royal Palm Beach, FL 33411

or email sonblock@clearlightcoms.com